When Stories Clash:

ADDRESSING CONFLICT WITH
NARRATIVE MEDIATION

Gerald Monk & John Winslade

WHEN STORIES CLASH:
Addressing Conflict with Narrative Mediation

The Cover: The photo on the front cover of this book is of what is known in New Zealand as a koru, or unfolding fern. It is often used to symbolize development or growth. We use it here to represent the unfolding of a story. At first a story may be tightly wound but, in response to skilful questioning, it gradually unfolds to a vibrant life.

Photo: John Winslade
Book Design: Debbi Stocco, debbistocco.com

Library of Congress Catalog Card Number: 2012950904

Taos Institute Publications
A Division of the Taos Institute
Chagrin Falls, Ohio
USA

ISBN 13: 978-1-938552-01-4

ISBN 10: 1-938552-01-6   PRINTED IN THE USA AND IN THE UK

Introduction to
Taos Institute Publications

The Taos Institute is a nonprofit organization dedicated to the development of social constructionist theory and practice for purposes of world benefit. Constructionist theory and practice locate the source of meaning, value, and action in communicative relations among people. Our major investment is in fostering relational processes that can enhance the welfare of people and the world in which they live. Taos Institute Publications offers contributions to cutting-edge theory and practice in social construction. Our books are designed for scholars, practitioners, students, and the openly curious public. The Focus Book Series provides brief introductions and overviews that illuminate theories, concepts, and useful practices. The Tempo Book Series is especially dedicated to the general public and to practitioners. The Books for Professionals Series provides in-depth works that focus on recent developments in theory and practice. Our books are particularly relevant to social scientists and to practitioners concerned with individual, family, organizational, community, and societal change.

—Kenneth J. Gergen
President, Board of Directors,
The Taos Institute

Taos Institute Board of Directors

Harlene Anderson   Sally St. George
David Cooperrider, Honorary   Jane Watkins, Honorary
Robert Cottor   Jason Wolf
Kenneth J. Gergen   Dan Wulff
Mary Gergen   Diana Whitney, Emerita
Sheila McNamee

Books for Professional Series Editor
Kenneth J. Gergen
Tempo Series Editor
Mary Gergen
Focus Book Series Editors
Harlene Anderson, Jane Seiling and Jackie Stavros
Executive Director
Dawn Dole

For information about the Taos Institute and social constructionism visit:
www.taosinstitute.com

Taos Institute Publications
Focus Book Series

When Stories Clash: Addressing Conflict with Narrative Mediation, (2013) by Gerald Monk, and John Winslade

Bereavement Support Groups: Breathing Life into Stories of the Dead, (2012) by Lorraine Hedtke

The Appreciative Organization, Revised Edition (2008) by Harlene Anderson, David Cooperrider, Kenneth J. Gergen, Mary Gergen, Sheila McNamee, Jane Watkins, and Diana Whitney

Appreciative Inquiry: A Positive Approach to Building Cooperative Capacity, (2005) by Frank Barrett and Ronald Fry

Dynamic Relationships: Unleashing the Power of Appreciative Inquiry in Daily Living, (2005) by Jacqueline Stavros and Cheri B. Torres

Appreciative Sharing of Knowledge: Leveraging Knowledge Management for Strategic Change, (2004) by Tojo Thatchenkery

Social Construction: Entering the Dialogue, (2004) by Kenneth J. Gergen, and Mary Gergen

Appreciative Leaders: In the Eye of the Beholder, (2001) edited by Marge Schiller, Bea Mah Holland, and Deanna Riley

Experience AI: A Practitioner's Guide to Integrating Appreciative Inquiry and Experiential Learning, (2001) by Miriam Ricketts and Jim Willis

Taos Tempo Series:
Collaborative Practices for Changing Times

Developing Relational Leadership: Resources for Developing Reflexive Organizational Practices, (2012) by Carsten Hornstrup, Jesper Loehr-Petersen, Joergen Gjengedal Madsen, Thomas Johansen, Allan Vinther Jensen

Practicing Relational Ethics in Organizations, (2012) by Gitte Haslebo and Maja Loua Haslebo

Healing Conversations Now: Enhance Relationships with Elders and Dying Loved Ones, (2011) by Joan Chadbourne and Tony Silbert

Riding the Current: How to Deal with the Daily Deluge of Data, (2010) by Madelyn Blair

Ordinary Life Therapy: Experiences from a Collaborative Systemic Practice, (2009) by Carina Håkansson

Mapping Dialogue: Essential Tools for Social Change, (2008) by Marianne "Mille" Bojer, Heiko Roehl, Mariane Knuth-Hollesen, and Colleen Magner

Positive Family Dynamics: Appreciative Inquiry Questions to Bring Out the Best in Families, (2008) by Dawn Cooperrider Dole, Jen Hetzel Silbert, Ada Jo Mann, and Diana Whitney

Books for Professionals Series

New Horizons in Buddhist Psychology: Relational Buddhism for Collaborative Practitioners, (2010) edited by Maurits G.T. Kwee

Positive Approaches to Peacebuilding: A Resource for Innovators, (2010) edited by Cynthia Sampson, Mohammed Abu-Nimer, Claudia Liebler, and Diana Whitney

Social Construction on the Edge: 'Withness'-Thinking & Embodiment, (2010) by John Shotter

Joined Imagination: Writing and Language in Therapy, (2009) by Peggy Penn

Celebrating the Other: A Dialogic Account of Human Nature, (reprint 2008) by Edward Sampson

Conversational Realities Revisited: Life, Language, Body and World, (2008) by John Shotter

Horizons in Buddhist Psychology: Practice, Research and Theory, (2006) edited by Maurits Kwee, Kenneth J. Gergen, and Fusako Koshikawa

Therapeutic Realities: Collaboration, Oppression and Relational Flow, (2005) by Kenneth J. Gergen

SocioDynamic Counselling: A Practical Guide to Meaning Making, (2004) by R. Vance Peavy

Experiential Exercises in Social Construction—A Fieldbook for Creating Change, (2004) by Robert Cottor, Alan Asher, Judith Levin, and Cindy Weiser

Dialogues About a New Psychology, (2004) by Jan Smedslund

For book information and ordering, visit Taos Institute Publications at:
www.taosinstitutepublications.net
For further information, call: 1-888-999-TAOS, 1-440-338-6733
Email: info@taosinstitute.net

Table of Contents

PREFACE

W E WROTE THIS BOOK TO be brief enough to read in one sitting. It is about the practice of narrative mediation. [1]In this text, we describe how to use our ideas in various conflict resolution contexts. Our focus is more on the how of narrative mediation than the why. We aim to provide a concise, yet rich description in words of many moments of practice in mediation, conflict coaching and conferencing and we can point out the intentions behind practice moves.

We also illustrate the practice with stories from family mediation, organizational disputes, restorative conferencing in schools, medical error conflicts in healthcare, and more. Along the way, we specify many questions we have found fruitful and recomend these as practical lines of inquiry.

---

1. Our first book on mediation (Winslade & Monk, 2000) articulated a practice and situated it in a philosophical framework. Our second book (Winslade & Monk, 2008) extended the theory of narrative mediation and pushed it into a variety of practice domains.

WHAT IS NARRATIVE MEDIATION?

Narrative mediation is based on the idea that disputes often catch people up in a conflict story that is painful and disturbing. They would prefer the relationship with the other person to be in a different place. Narrative mediation helps to separate people from the conflict story and to develop a story of the relationship they would prefer. The aim is to assist people to overcome the divisiveness of a conflict by working to identify the conflict story and growing a counter story that opens up possibilities to make things as right as possible.

We assume that people give coherence to their lives and relationships by developing stories about them. We therefore privilege stories and the meanings within stories over facts and causes. Conflicts between individuals or groups are impacted by the wider social forces that give shape to the stories by which we live. Any story is a selection from available plot events and any relationship can support multiple stories. There is thus always a counter story that can be found.

Double listening, deconstructive inquiry and externalizing conversation (all explained in subsequent chapters) loosen the authority of dominant conflict stories and make room for oft-neglected counter stories to emerge from the shadows. Non-conflictual moments can then be woven into a viable counter story through connecting them together. The goals are: a) to create the relational conditions for the growth of a story of cooperation in the face of conflict; b) to build a story of relationship that is incompatible with the continuing dominance of conflict; and c) to open space for people to make changes and to negotiate new understandings.

How to achieve these goals is the focus of this book. Chapters in the book are arranged to mirror the sequential application of skills. Chapter one introduces the practice. Chapter two emphasizes listening to conflict stories as points of intersection of cultural forces. Chapter three focuses on the skill of double listening. Chapter four is about building externalizing conversations that separate persons from problems. Chapter five shows how to find openings to a counter story. Chapter six describes how to grow a counter story into a viable basis for going forward. Finally, chapter seven draws the threads together in a conclusion.

Our thanks are owed to those who have made this book possible. Ken Gergen provided initial encouragement to write this text. Dawn Dole has managed the production process and helpful editing was provided by Mary Gergen, Harlene Anderson and Bob Cotter. Their contributions are much appreciated. We also thank Saskia Boom for her additions and thorough page proofing.

Our hope now is that readers will look within these pages for practices they can immediately use and will take heart from our stories in the growth of their own versions of narrative practice[2].

Gerald Monk and John Winslade
California, August, 2012

---

2. The photo on the front cover of this book is of what is known in New Zealand as a koru, or unfolding fern. It is often used to symbolize development or growth. We use it here to represent the unfolding of a story. At first a story may be tightly wound but, in response to skillful questioning, it gradually unfolds to a vibrant life. Photo by John Winslade

Chapter 1
Introducing the Practice

BEVAN, A FORTY-ONE YEAR OLD man, checked into the emergency room after a negative reaction to some seafood he had eaten an hour before. His tongue and face had swollen. Suffering from a serious allergic reaction, he was treated with a dose of epinephrine.

Bevan began showing signs of improvement but was held for observation. Then some of his symptoms returned. A second dose of epinephrine was administered—a typical procedure to relieve ongoing symptoms of the allergic reaction.

A short while later, Bevan started to experience chest pain and shortness of breath. His vital signs began deteriorating. The emergency doctor, Dr. Garland, reviewed the chart and discovered that Bevan had been injected with ten times the recommended amount of the adrenaline hormone—an overdose that had nearly killed him. His near death resulting from the high dosage caused permanent heart damage, which was severe enough to place Bevan on a waitlist for a heart transplant.

Bevan's family and friends were incredulous. They struggled to make sense of what had happened. At one moment Bevan had been having dinner with them and a few hours later he had nearly died and now they were learning that he was facing permanent impairment as a result of a gross mistake by a healthcare professional. One does not need to be especially discerning to see that this situation was heading toward a showdown between Bevan and his family and the hospital and its medical staff.

We shall return to the story shortly but first let us pause to notice that these events cannot be adequately understood as simply individual phenomena. They happen in a cultural context. Even in the face of tremendous human tragedy it is possible to identify background cultural narratives at work, producing human interactions that become the source of conflict. A healthcare system is a site where various cultural forces intersect and shape personal responses and interpersonal conflict in particular formats. We shall provide an analysis of some of these cultural forces, as well as showcase the implementation of narrative mediation practices in a high stakes context.

In the early 21st century, many people have grown up with the assumption that the hospital is a place where sick people can be healed. Strong ideas about trusting nurses and doctors to care for us circulate in our communities. We learn from multiple sources that doctors and nurses will work tirelessly for a cure and that modern medicine can work miracles. We expect to be treated with the best of care, backed up with the latest scientific knowledge and evidence-based practices. Where do we learn these ideas?

The answer is that we soak up these ideas from stories in the movies, television soap operas, and documentaries; from studying reports of research; from firsthand accounts of family members or from our own lived experience of doctors and hospitals. In other words, we inform ourselves by drawing from what Michel Foucault (1989) referred to as the *great anonymous murmur of discourse* (p. 27).

In the United States, hospitals vie with one another for consumers of competing healthcare plans. A recent publicity campaign by a large healthcare system promised patients and their families 'clinical excellence', 'the highest-quality patient care', to 'do the right thing every day' and to be the 'best healthcare provider in the universe!' Another healthcare system promises 'to make life better' for people. Many healthcare providers lay claim to ethical standards of integrity, honesty and trustworthiness or promise to represent 'model quality health care' as the 'best place to receive care'. Such is the background 'murmur' of healthcare discourse.

These advertising campaigns strengthen the cultural narratives about high quality and safe service provision for those who are sick. As we internalize these cultural narratives, they influence our expectations and shape what we say, how we feel, and what we do when interacting with healthcare systems.

Yet despite the vigorous promises of healing narratives, inadvertent harm is done to patients on a regular basis. When the background assumptions of care are violated, patients experience not only damage to their functioning but also a sense of personal betrayal by doctors and nurses.

'You promised you would care for me but you didn't!'

Such harm is more common in hospitals than most of us are prepared to acknowledge. Hospital errors in the United States are between the fifth and eighth leading causes of death (Kohn, Corrigan, & Donaldson, 2000). Deaths from medical errors are reported to be higher among Americans than breast cancer, traffic accidents or AIDS. Kohn et. al. also reported a stunning five to ten percent of patients who enter a hospital will be subjected to medical error. Family members of those who suffer catastrophic outcomes struggle to make sense of the contrast between the promise of care on the one hand, and the real suffering caused by inadvertent harm on the other.

Bevan's family members, especially his wife and his father, were flooded with shock, rage and despair. They could not come to terms with what had happened to their son and husband they had entrusted into the hands of healthcare professionals, whose job it was to make Bevan better. They were now caught in a spiraling and despairing round of what seemed like an irresolvable conflict with their healthcare provider. Their friends were already talking about taking the hospital, and the staff involved, to court.

But it is not just the patients who are affected by the 'murmur' of discourse. Medical professionals too are influenced by these cultural forces. They are trained in medical schools and in hospital residencies to be perfectionist in their delivery of healthcare and not to make mistakes. When doctors and nurses cause catastrophic, or even less serious but still unanticipated, preventable errors, the effects can be devastating. Many physicians process these events by believing they have failed the patient, starting to second-guess their clinical skills or their knowledge base, and even questioning their career choice. Wu (2007) captures the intensity of a physician's reaction, when confronted with violating the Hippocratic Oath of abstaining from doing harm.

'Virtually every practitioner knows the sickening realization of making a bad mistake ... You know you should confess, but dread the prospect of potential punishment and of the patient's anger. You may become overly attentive to the patient or family, lamenting the failure to do so earlier and, if you have not told them, wondering if they know.' (pp. 726-727).

The physician involved in the incident of the epinephrine overdose was plagued by this dread of medical error and of the accompanying encounter with the wrath of a family. Dr. Garland wanted help to process the events and also needed an opportunity to address the crisis unfolding with Bevan and his family.

Narrative mediators are not only interested in helping disputing parties reach agreement as a possible outcome of mediation. More importantly, the mediator is interested in building a narrative that features shared understandings and some movement towards mutual respect. On these bases, agreements and courses of action might be decided upon.

A narrative analysis of conflict avoids an exclusive focus on individual actions, expectations and interests. It also implicates the background cultural assumptions, or discourses, that inform people's understandings of what is acceptable, normal, right, or possible. Making the social and cultural world visible influences how conflicts can be thought of and helps the parties find a pathway forward. This element of narrative mediation contrasts with some other mediation practices that focus on the internal individual processes of motivation, identifies parties' underlying interests, and works for resolution, often without reference to the cultural universe in which individual interests lie.

In this next section we lay out some key elements of narrative mediation. These fundamentals will be distinguished from other forms of mediation. The discussion will take place in direct reference to the conflict with which we opened the chapter.

AN ETHICAL STANCE

A narrative mediator recognizes that there are powerful forces operating in all conflict situations. This includes the cultural narratives that shape the mediator's responses as well. As a result, ethics of impartiality, neutrality and objectivity, dimensions deemed essential for the mediator by many mediation models, cannot be realized in practice. Mediators are pulled in different directions by the cultural threads being played out in the conflict. A mediator cannot have a neutral reaction to the despair that the family must feel when their loved one is severely damaged by such a grievous act. Mediators are also family members and medical patients.

Neither can a mediator remain unaffected by the professional positioning that shapes a doctor's responses. Mediators are also professionals. They can appreciate on a personal level the fear and self-criticism that a physician may experience when facing an angry family intent on pursuing litigation.

Mediators are also influenced by the gaze of the employer who is funding their mediation practice. In some healthcare contexts, mediators are employed by healthcare providers to help settle healthcare disputes. They may help families access the services they need and address problems causing distress. They may also be expected by job descriptions to stop conflicts from spiraling out of control into expensive litigation.

While mediators cannot be neutral, objective or unaffected in their responses, neither can they give themselves license to deliberately favor one party over another. At the very least, they must work to be even-handed. Sometimes this means working hard to be curious about and understand more fully the concerns of someone who is different in some way from the mediator. The ethic that is more useful here than neutrality is reflexivity. It suggests making oneself accountable to a person for how well one understands them. For example, a mediator might ask from time to time, 'How am I doing at making sense of what you are saying?' Being mindful of the background cultural forces pulling in various directions can actually help a mediator remain respectful of all parties' concerns.

In narrative mediation we are also careful to avoid attributing the conflict to any kind of essential deficit in either party.

The profound respect involved in avoiding deficit thinking means taking people seriously, rather than interpreting them in terms of pathology such as mental illness. This means consistently working from the assumption that, the person is not the problem; the problem is the problem (White, 1989, p. 6).

In the example we are using, the mediator pays attention to the patient's and the family's concerns as well as to the doctor's concerns. He also expresses curiosity about the cultural forces at work in producing these concerns. Throughout this process, the mediator constantly checks how his responses might be shaped by cultural narratives.

The space where the mediation happens is also a discursive space that carries cultural meanings. For example, Bevan's family may experience strong reactions and some degree of intimidation, if required to meet with the physician at the same hospital where the tragedy occurred. A setting comfortable to both the family and the physician would be imperative in creating an environment conducive to an even-handed approach.

MEETING SEPARATELY WITH THE PARTIES IN CONFLICT

Narrative mediators almost always prefer to meet parties separately for the first time and then periodically conduct separate sessions to address concerns that are best addressed privately. By contrast, some mediation approaches are emphatic about only meeting with the parties in a joint session to showcase neutrality and openness. However, our experience is that starting with separate sessions leads to much more favorable outcomes.

For example, it would be important to hold separate meetings with the patient, Bevan, and his family, and at another time with the physician. In these meetings the mediator can seek to clearly understand and become familiar with the emotional effects of the issue. Dr. Garland also would be unlikely to be able to discuss the impact of this catastrophic event on his own life and career in front of the angry family members. He would very likely need a separate session to organize his thoughts on how to express his sorrow and how to explain what had happened without further escalating the family's distress.

The separate meetings also provide the mediator with first hand knowledge of the nuanced concerns that are not always expressed in joint sessions. Sensitive and private information can be shared in such meetings that could not be risked in front of others with whom one is in conflict, for fear of giving them further ammunition with which to be hurtful. The mediator can also elicit any resources and strengths of the parties that might become useful in the joint mediation sessions to build under-standings and agreements. Perhaps most importantly, separate meetings create an opportunity for the mediator and the parties to build trust and understanding. The mediator can show that he cares about the distress people have experienced and the concerns they are motivated by. Mediators can also demonstrate a strong grasp of the specific issues the parties have been affected by.

The issues experienced by Bevan and his family:

- Their trust in a doctor who was supposed to help Bevan has been violated by the doctor's actions, which nearly killed Bevan.

- They have a desire for justice and for the hospital and the doctor to be held accountable.
- Coping with Bevan's day-to-day struggles to survive is producing associated stresses: lack of sleep, financial challenges, relational strains.
- They have substantial fears about Bevan's future and a potential early death.
- They experience waves of desire for vengeance and retribution.

The issues experienced by Dr. Garland:

- He has lost much professional confidence and is battling a personal sense of failure.
- Depression is also accompanying the sense of failure.
- Fear of facing Bevan's family and their anger is debilitating him.
- Worry about how to express to the family his deep regret over what happened dogs him every day.

The mediator conducts an externalizing conversation (see chapter 4) with both parties independently to name the issues that are troubling them and to define their effects. In this conversation, the mediator explores the emotional landscape surrounding the conflict, as well as considers the possible concerns underlying what the parties want to address. After identifying whether the parties do in fact want to meet together, they are also asked to explicitly state what they would like to address and to achieve in the joint sessions that will follow. Each of the parties might be asked:

At the end of the joint meeting, what would you like to have accomplished? What would make it feel like the meeting had been worthwhile?

What would tell you that the meeting had helped things move forward?

These conversations at the end of the separate meetings help the parties to:

- calibrate whether their expectations are realistic about what might be achieved.
- connect with and clarify their desired outcomes.
- examine the cultural discourses that might be impinging on their desired outcomes.
- clarify the values, hopes and desires they want to keep to the fore as they conduct themselves in the joint session, especially when the conversation threatens to be captured by problem-saturated conversations.

Bevan's family's main concerns were twofold. First, they wanted to find ways to move on and not be paralyzed by distress and fear. Secondly, they wanted to hold the doctor and hospital accountable and to have them repay the family in some way.

Dr. Garland's main concern was to try to put this tragedy behind him and have the family compensated. He was willing to offer a heartfelt apology. He hoped either to regain his confidence and practice medicine again or to leave the profession altogether and start over in some other occupation. These individual sessions prepared the parties for the first joint session.

FIRST JOINT SESSION

From a narrative orientation, the mediation process will start, as in many other mediation approaches, with the mediator providing some structure to the joint meeting. The mediator outlines her role as facilitator of conversation between the parties so that greater understanding can be achieved and movement towards some preferred outcome can be sought. The mediator explains she is not a judge who will direct the parties to particular courses of action. Neither will the mediator pronounce some decision on whose perspective is more valid or true. The narrative practitioner takes pains to be clear that it is the parties who will have opportunity to realize their stated hopes (outlined in the separate sessions) by building greater understanding about the challenging issues that have brought about the conflict.

Narrative mediation places greater emphasis on building shared understandings in alignment with people's stated goals than on reaching a specific, detailed agreement as the guiding mission. In the scenario discussed above, the suffering, violation, and betrayal experienced by Bevan and his family is not going to be settled by an agreement on things that can be agreed upon (like monetary compensation). In the mediation, the family first and foremost wants a human response to their suffering. The most potent thing that Dr. Garland might do for this family is to express a heartfelt acknowledgement of their suffering and to indicate that he is also devastated by what happened.

It is the quality of the relational climate that is crucial to promoting the changes necessary to address the concerns of the parties in this scenario. The emphasis is on the careful development of a respectful and safe relational space to address issues and to avoid moving too quickly to specific content items. It would be more risky for mediators to revert to a laborious brain-storming exchange in an aversive relational climate. While, in some contexts, narrative practitioners are not averse to focusing on specific concrete possibilities through brain-storming strategies, the mediator does not start off mediation in this way. The primary focus is on the production of a story of relationship that might contain the necessary conversation for the purpose of increased understanding.

The mediator had already ascertained from the separate meetings that Bevan and his family wanted an apology, some acknowledgment of their suffering, and to make sure that this doctor and this healthcare system could never do this to anybody else. It was the acknowledgment of suffering in this case that provided a pathway forward for this family. Because of the separate meeting with the hospital administration representative, the mediator already understood that the hospital would take responsibility for the harm done to Bevan, and was willing to explore ways to improve their systems of medication delivery. Such a stance can be an enormous step in the right direction for people in the position of Bevan and his family. On this basis the hospital could process a financial settlement that would meet the federal and state guidelines for settlement of harm of this magnitude.

Narrative mediators engage where possible with all parties in the development of some ongoing narrative. Dr. Garland benefits from having an outlet for the expression of his grief and distress at the medical error, rather than resorting to a 'hide-and-defend' approach. The terrible isolation that follows such a strategy is typical of traditional approaches to dealing with medical error. The narrative mediator has at her disposal a powerful array of mediation tools to move productively through perhaps even three or four joint mediation sessions that ultimately produce the best possible mutual understandings and shared ideas about how to move forward. These mediation tools and techniques are elaborated in the following chapters of this book. They include *double listening, externalizing and mapping the effects of a conflict, building stories of cooperation, and generating understanding as a basis for knowing how to go on.*

MEDIATION AND CONSTRUCTIONISM

Narrative mediation is not just a set of tools and techniques without substance and rationale. It is grounded in a robust set of ideas. It embodies in practice a theoretical foundation drawn from several movements of thought, including narrative theory, feminist politics, poststructuralism, and social constructionist psychology. Constructionism (Berger, & Luckmann, 1966; Burr, 2003; Gergen, 2009) emphasizes the cultural context of the person rather than a universal foundational psychology of the individual and the family. It assumes that we are both bearers of and also reproducers of the cultural patterns that we have learned throughout our lives. From this perspective, culture is not like a layer of chocolate coating around a person's individual nature but is as fundamental as biology to every aspect of who each person is and how each person responds to others.

The exchanges between Bevan and his family and the hospital representatives, including Dr. Garland, go beyond mere expressions of individual interests or solely personal emotional experiences. A social constructionist orientation directs us to understand how each person's responses are produced out of the forces at work between people. These forces include the ways in which people seek to influence (or succeed in influencing) each other or the ways in which attempts to influence each other break down into conflict. Any relation of mutual influence is in this sense a power relation. Power relations are understood by constructionist and postmodern researchers and commentators such as Foucault (1980; 2000), Bruner (1986), Lyotard (1984) and Davies and Harré (1990) to be shaped by pervasive social and psychological norms, events that effect changes in narrative trajectories and the positioning influences of dominating dis-courses. However, this constructionist analysis also pays atten-tion to the abilities of parties to differentiate themselves from dominant cultural assumptions and come to creative solutions to address culturally produced conflicts. Consideration of this larger picture does not have to make mediation too complex to make a difference. It can do the opposite and turn complexity into multiple possibilities. That is what the rest of this book seeks to articulate—how to rescue stories of possibility from the jaws of conflict.

SUMMARY FOCUS

- Conflicts are not simply produced out of a clash of individual interests. They are also products of cultural forces.

- Individual interests often contain within them internalized elements of cultural forces.

- Narrative mediation is focused on building relational narratives of increased understanding, respect and cooperation, out of which agreements, if needed, can be fashioned.

- The goal of mediation is not just to reach agreement but to help people determine a pathway forward.

- Neutrality and impartiality are not realistic ethical goals for mediators.

- A more useful ethical principle is to practice in a reflexive way and to seek to remain accountable to the parties for the mediator's inevitable biases.

- Narrative practice is built on the assumption that, 'The person is not the problem; the problem is the problem.'

- Wherever possible, we prefer to meet with parties separately before a joint mediation meeting.

- Narrative mediation is built on the constructionist assumption that people's responses in conflict situations are formed out of the forces at work between people.

- Conflict always involves a power relation.

- Complexity is an ally rather than an obstacle for narrative practice because it always provides other possible pathways of response.

CHAPTER 2
CULTURE AND CONFLICT

RECENTLY, I (GERALD) CROSSED THE USA border through St. Thomas, (a beautiful Caribbean island) after a vacation on a nearby island. As anyone who has traveled to the United States in the post-September 11 world will know, it is quite an ordeal going through American security, passport control, immigration and customs. Regular air travelers know the ritual of taking off their jackets, shoes, belts, and then organizing cell phones, wallets and computers in the plastic trays that go through the security x-ray machine. I have completed this cultural ritual on dozens of occasions every year. Those who are new to the ritual of U.S. security will often get quite flustered, become confused about what they are supposed to do, and take some time to figure out what is expected of them.

In the long lines that form around security checkpoints the tension can grow when people take a minute or two to situate themselves and work out what they need to do. When immigration officials identify somebody holding up a line, the security officer will usher people to move around such individuals to keep the line moving in order to de-escalate tensions in this stressful location.

Now, in St. Thomas, the line was quite long. I could see that the individual ahead of me had probably never gone through a U.S. security checkpoint. After what seemed like a few minutes waiting for this individual, I thought I would do the right thing and pass the disoriented and preoccupied flyer, who was oblivious to the frustrated travelers waiting behind him. I expected the security officer to appreciate my help to quickly move past the stalled individual to keep the line moving. At this stage of proceedings, there was only the security officer between me and the x-ray machine. I moved towards the x-ray machine, expecting the officer to wave me forward.

Instead, she held up her hand and in a strong voice said, 'Stand back!' She had witnessed my maneuver and said in a somewhat aggressive and commanding tone, 'Stand over there!'

I was aware in this moment of 'a line of force' (a term coined by philosopher Gilles Deleuze, 1988) running through our interaction. I was in a power relation with the security officer but there was a line of authority that stretched back behind her commanding tone all the way to the US government. I could certainly challenge this authority but knew that any force I could muster behind my response would be unlikely to match the strength of the line of force behind her words. I chose discretion and demurred.

I was now waiting in front of the x-ray machine but was not being permitted to go through it. Time passed and the disoriented traveler finally was motioned to go through the x-ray machine. The officer stood under a large sign posted by the Department of Homeland Security that said something like, 'All passengers have a right to receive professional and courteous treatment.'

She held me a little longer, and then I was finally ushered through. In that moment, I felt disrespected and angry. I was upset because I had been trying to be an obedient and compliant traveler by keeping the line moving and upset too because the officer had used an aggressive tone of voice with me, apparently violating her own professional code of conduct. When I was gathering my belongings off the conveyor belt, this very same officer was close enough for me to speak.

I was going to say to her, 'Why were you so rude and aggressive?' knowing at this point that I was on the right side of the x-ray machine. Instead, I thought to say, barely containing my contempt, 'I am curious why you had me stand to one side, not allowing me to go through the x-ray machine, when clearly there was no one in front of me.'

She responded with calm composure, 'Sir, it is important that people don't jump the line. Manners are important here.'

My private fuming was quickly disarmed by this comment. We had produced two completely different meanings about the security ritual by which we were bound together. I had seen her as rigid and punitive in the application of power bestowed upon her by a line of force originating in a vast and powerful security system. She saw me as an ill-mannered, entitled traveler who had violated a cultural norm of politeness by jumping the line. Doubtless she sees many people every day who express their sense of superior entitlement in various ways and treat her as a lowly employee in a menial job. There was thus another possible line of force running through the situation that apparently lay behind her response to me. It originates perhaps more in social class difference than in state authority. These and other possible lines of force were intersecting at this moment. As a result, neither of us was conforming to one another's expectations about the respectful and right thing to do.

This story serves as a starting point to tease out the underpinnings of conflict from the perspective of narrative mediation. Small day-to-day events of this kind can illustrate the application of a narrative lens in understanding the nature and source of conflict in human systems. In particular, the actions of the security officer and of myself cannot be adequately understood as founded solely on our individual interests, motivations, beliefs or values. We are participating in an exchange formed at the point of intersection of complex cultural forces that do not originate with either of us as individuals. To say this is not so much to point to the cultural categories of belonging that each of us represent, although that may sometimes be relevant. It is rather to start from the assumption that culture is best thought of in terms of practices held in place by cultural narratives and that these cultural narratives are shot through with power (or lines of force) of various kinds.

This viewpoint is, however, a relatively recent development in the understanding of culture. It grows out of some philosophical shifts introduced through the constructionist worldview. From this perspective, culture is better understood as the constantly shifting process by which people actively give meaning to things and about how competing narrative trajectories interact in the moment. It is less about a static set of ready-made assumptions about how a particular category of people might be expected to respond. See Monk, Winslade, & Sinclair (2008) for a fuller account of this perspective.

The cultural rituals around securing the borders of a country provide a rich context for understanding a small conflict story through a narrative lens. The job of security personnel at international borders is to examine both the legitimacy and potential threat of travelers entering a country. Their task is to scrutinize the behavior of a potential security threat. In addition, security personnel participate in the production of security surveillance according to norms that define an efficient and well-organized system. As a system of surveillance on behalf of the state the security procedure fits with what Michel Foucault (1980, 2000) analyzed as a practice of *modern power*.

As a regular traveler, I am acutely aware of these security parameters. I know my job is to establish my legitimacy, demonstrate personal orderliness and perform conformity to the security rituals. Normally, I submit to expected requirements as I move through these cultural rituals in a rather seamless fashion in order to minimize potential conflict. What I had not calibrated my demeanor to accommodate in this exotic Caribbean border location was the wide embrace by Caribbean security officials of a slower and more convivial pacing in human activity. By jumping the line I had failed to conform to the cultural expectations of being patient, moving slowly, and thus demonstrating courtesy. Instead of labeling the security officer as a power-hungry and officious agent of the state, I could have understood this individual as upholding specific security traditions and as a guardian of a quite distinct, local, social practice in this security context. Rather than my own behavior being interpreted as an act of defiance, selfishness and impoliteness, it could have been understood as a willingness to conform and preserve orderliness by keeping the line moving-behaviors deemed appropriate in most other U.S. security contexts, but out of place in this specific cultural context.

The conflict arose because these two distinct cultural forces that intersected in this moment were internalized in the assumptions of the two protagonists, and were expressed in their actions. Both people were positioned by the background cultural narratives in a clash of meanings. Examining conflict from a social and cultural perspective provides a language with which to name the particular social processes operating on parties in conflict. Appreciating the cultural forces produced by competing narratives, or discourses, also provides a way forward in negotiation and mediation without resorting to blaming talk.

Small conflictual conversations or large-scale community conflicts arise because cultural violations have occurred. Sometimes
these result from wholesale practices of domination, but not
always. In Western contexts, most people prefer non-conflictual
lives but from time to time find themselves caught up in conflicts
without quite knowing how they got there. In order to comfort-
ably maneuver through the daily challenges of life and diminish
the level of conflict, most of us respond favorably to predictability
and agreement. We like it when people follow the protocols that
seem right to us. In the West, we like people to say 'please' and
'thank you', or to say 'bless you' when someone sneezes. When
people do not show these social niceties, we quickly judge them
as possessing some kind of deficit. In a business greeting, we like
an introductory firm handshake, but not too firm. When we eat,
we like people to conform to 'right conduct' around food preparation, the serving of food and the eating of it. In the United States,
there are highly developed cultural norms about what is correct
eating etiquette and good service in a restaurant. Generally, most
restaurant-goers like the waiter or waitress to come quickly to
the table and ask whether or not the patrons would like a drink.
Glasses of water should continuously be refilled. Napkins should
be readily available. In a good restaurant the server should come
to the table regularly to check whether the customers are doing
well and should be compliant to the customers' needs. There are
particular expectations about the quality of the food and the way
it is served. What is defined as good service in a restaurant seems
to be obvious, even common sense, to many. If it is not good ser-

vice, the cultural sanction is to complain to the manager or with-hold or reduce the size of the tip.

Lack of conformity to these, sometimes nuanced, traditions is quickly interpreted as disrespect, rudeness or poor service and can certainly become fodder for a conflictual experience. Customer service expectations are cultural assumptions and norms are easily converted to customer rights and restaurant owner responsibilities.

In this way, we develop elaborate notions of what are every-day truths, based upon dominant cultural practices. However, the realities of our lives show that our everyday truths are frequently challenged or violated in some way. It does not take much for this to happen, as outlined above. Taken-for-granted assumptions about common courtesy and appropriate conduct are easily violated in contexts where there are a richer range of cultural forces in play.

Human communities form highly structured and specific systems of thought that define what will be considered respectful, well-mannered, fair and just. These customs vary considerably from place to place. In one community, spitting in the street is a benign act; in another community it is viewed as uncouth and primitive. Refraining from honking one's car horn, standing in line, and waiting for the cross signal to sound before a pedestrian crosses the road are viewed as modeling good citizenship in one ethnic community. In another community, consistently honking one's horn, shuffling forward in a crowd and listening to the cross signal as a suggestion, rather than a command, are viewed as sensible, normal and right ways to live. When these cultural norms collide in a multi-ethnic and culturally diverse community, it is easy to ignore the background cultural norms and traditions that invite and reinforce particular human actions. Instead, when people witness the defilement of what counts to them as 'common sense', they can start to view others as transgressors, who can be easily labeled as deficient, sick, ignorant, uneducated, evil or just wrong.

Historically, the social sciences have emphasized individualism over the cultural processes of social construction in understanding how people act. From a constructionist perspective, individuals are not unitary creations who operate independently. The anthropologist Clifford Geertz (1983) stated that most world cultures view the Western idea of the uniqueness and separateness of the person, independent from their social and cultural background, as a peculiar idea. Emphasis on the unitary nature of human beings has nevertheless dominated the Western world in the last two hundred years and has shaped the major social science disciplines. It has also strongly influenced the mediation field. The most well-known mediation model in North America is the interest-based mediation approach (Fisher, Ury, & Patton, 2011; Moore, 1996) which rests upon an individualistic analysis of human behavior. From this standpoint, conflict is thought to result from the thwarting of a natural human drive to fulfill needs, and so the task of the mediator becomes to help disputants remove obstacles to need satisfaction through the creation of win-win solutions.

At this juncture, let us review some of the concepts we have discussed and summarize the key points conveyed.

- Conflicts are produced out of the background cultural narratives that influence people in particular ways.

- Culture, rather than inner forces arising solely from within individuals, constructs people's attitudes, feelings, positions, and interests.

- Dominant cultural stories shape people's attitudes, beliefs, and identities.

- Out of these dominant stories, lines of force run through our interactions with others.

- It is more useful to think of people as constantly making nuanced decisions that are shaped by competing cultural narratives, or lines of force, than to think of them as belonging to categories of persons with predictable simple cultural patterns of response (even if these are moderated by personal idiosyncrasies).

THE MEDIATOR AND CULTURAL LOCATION

From a constructionist framework, mediation is a provisional activity and cannot claim to provide an impartial and essential step-by-step guide that promises a secure outcome for participating disputants. A mediator has to embrace ambiguity and indeterminacy in an escalating conflict and nurture a spirit of informed curiosity about what is unfolding (Winslade, & Monk, 2000; 2008). From this perspective, there are no universal, truth-based approaches to rely on as justifications for the mediator's actions. This ambiguity provokes a moral dilemma for the mediator. Like the disputing parties, the mediator cannot avoid being positioned in a particular cultural location in the conflict, even as he or she is mediating it. There is no privileged position outside of this cultural location from which one can speak.

Each time mediators open their mouths and choose certain expressions over others, they choose one set of positions and not others. In this sense mediators are never neutral, as conventional mediation theory requires. So the important question is not so much whether the mediator is neutral with regard to the content of the dispute. Instead it is crucial that the mediator remain open about which cultural location and moral position he or she will work from and how accountable for the limits of that approach the mediator will make himself or herself. A constructionist perspective acknowledges that mediators are acting from an ethical value position or moral standpoint, rather than from a place of neutrality. From this standpoint mediators are better prepared to acknowledge how their ethical, moral, and professional stance will shape and influence the way in which the conflict will be addressed.

This analysis of the role of the mediator contrasts with the individualistic notion that the mediator can serve an impartial function. The reality is that cultural forces constantly influence the mediator, just as diverse cultural forces influence the conflicted parties seeking mediation. Nevertheless, the mediator must manage these social processes so that the parties are treated in an evenhanded and respectful manner.

RELATIONSHIP BETWEEN CULTURE AND NARRATIVE

Some people who come across narrative mediation for the first time assume that its focus is on merely the telling of stories of what has happened in the dispute, or on the analysis of the telling of such stories. Our work with narrative mediation has more to do with how narratives are shaping people's lives, including those that emanate from background cultural forces. We are interested in the stories that people tell about themselves or tell about each other and how these narratives establish a sense of identity, belonging and continuity in life. Stories give people a sense that life is not just a random series of events without rhyme or reason. Narratives produce a sense of coherence about who they are and who they are becoming, including who they are in a conflict. As Sara Cobb (1993; 2012) has pointed out, some narratives are more coherent accounts of life than others. Some retellings are more rehearsed than others. These differences influence what happens to the stories that people tell in the context of mediation.

Diverse cultural narratives are relevant because we do not construct personal stories in a vacuum. We draw from cultural information that is fashioned readymade to convey a particular set of viewpoints, produce specific affective states, render legitimate certain forms of explanation for past actions, and provide a rationale for future actions. Narrative elements are assembled through plot devices, and characters are assigned particular statuses, such as victim, villain, rescuer, saintly hero, objectified target, flawed genius, or powerful controller.

As narrative mediators observe these narrative elements at work, they pay attention to the background cultural scripts followed by the protagonists, without falling into the assumption that the participants are the original authors. Stock story lines come easily to mind of persons who might be characterized as the schoolyard bully, the controlling husband, the punitive boss, or the arrogant all-knowing physician. Disputants often fit themselves and their fellow disputants into well-known story lines and these become short-hand mechanisms through which people give an account of themselves and their conflict. These stock story lines are used to garner support and recognition from friends and family and most importantly from the person mediating the dispute.

CULTURE, NARRATIVE AND DISCOURSE

Narratives come with built-in assumptions about how the world is, how people should be, and how people should respond when the 'rules' are broken. We describe these ever present assumptions as *discourse*, a term conceptualized by Michel Foucault (1972, 1978, 1980, 2000). He emphasized the function of discourse as repetitive practice out of which people form their understandings of the world. These understandings then work in turn to inform the practices (both linguistic and behavioral) that people engage in. The motion of discourse is thus circular and works to seal off the possibility of thinking otherwise. Discourse is a function of the way that people use patterns of language to embody social norms and to establish taken-for-granted understandings about how things are in the world.

Discourses can be represented as statements of meaning about the ordinary and everyday aspects of life as we discussed above. Here are other examples:

- Eating fruit is good for you.
- It is polite to say thank you when offered something.
- Family loyalty is of primary importance.
- It is important to stand up for yourself when attacked.
- Hard work brings rewards.
- Infidelity ends a marriage.

Behind each of these statements lies a story that people have heard repeated many times or that they can slot into when life circumstances demand that they do so. Many of these pieces of discourse are not at all contentious, but some are strongly disputed, for example:

- A man should be the head of the household.
- White privilege is based on natural superiority.
- Homosexuality is not natural.
- Disabled persons should be grateful for the charity they receive.

Each of these meanings serves an organizing function in a power relation of domination. It sets up dividing lines in a social world and organizes exchanges between people as representatives of social groups. Notice how the word natural is used in some of these statements. It illustrates the way in which discourses work to make some assumptions appear to have such undisputed ordinariness that they can scarcely be questioned. They appear to be, and come to be treated as, part of the natural order of the universe.

Discourses, however, are products of human communities. They are not natural. We know that human communities are constantly shifting and changing too. So what seems like natural common sense today may be different tomorrow. Part of what produces change is the function of resistance. People frequently resist the force of a discourse, especially when it functions to set up dividing lines that are used as the basis for domination or the production of injustice.

Mediators need to be alert to expressions of resistance to dominant discourse within the conflict narratives with which they are regaled.

SUMMARY FOCUS

- Conflict narratives are made up of plots and characters organized according to themes in a coherent story.
- Themes, plots and characters are drawn from background cultural scripts.
- Conflict happens when others do not match our expectations, which are products of discourse.
- Discourses are building blocks of culture and can be represented as statements of meaning.
- Lines of force originating out of cultural narratives often intersect in moments of conflict.
- Power relations are established through discourse around dividing lines between groups of people.
- Mediators are never neutral with regard to the substantive content of disputes because they are also positioned by cultural discourse.
- Reflexivity and transparency are more important to narrative mediation than neutrality.
- Discourses are always subject to challenge and change.

CHAPTER 3
DOUBLE LISTENING

MEDIATORS ARE COMMONLY TAUGHT TO practice careful listening. What is usually being referred to are the skills and practices of *active listening*, especially paraphrasing and reflecting. These skills no doubt provide parties with the experience of being acknowledged for the emotional richness of what they say. What is seldom mentioned, however, is the idea that any piece of listening is necessarily selective as Westmark, Offenberg, & Nissen (2011) show. Recognition of this principle is foundational in social constructionism. There are multiple readings that can be made of any conflict and it matters which one(s) we listen to. In making such choices we play a significant role in the construction of a conversation and, therefore, in the eventual construction of people's lives.

Out of the many things that could be paid attention to, even the most active listening requires us to select out for attention some representation of the speaker's experience ahead of other possible candidates. Contextual forces play a role in this selection. For example, if someone consults a professional about a struggle to overcome a difficult conflict and happens to mention in passing a general contentment with a particular relationship, few listeners would abandon the exploration of the sources of conflict to spend an hour exploring the sense of contentment in this relationship. More troubled content would likely be selected for attention.

Because there is always a selection of what to focus on, good listening is not just a matter of process. Content also matters. In other words, it makes a difference just what we might listen for, rather than just how we might listen. It is therefore an axiom of narrative practice that we start from the assumption that conflict stories are always multiple stories. Obviously the two (or more) parties to a dispute will always have different stories to tell about what has happened. Their accounts will select out different facts, arrange them with different emphasis, and place them in a different order. But further than this, even one person's account can be heard as containing different stories. As they talk, people can be heard to actively rule out competing accounts and state their preferences for the account they want a listener to attend to.

For example, someone might say, 'You may think that I sound selfish when I say I want the children to stay mostly with me, but actually I am thinking of the children's best interests.'

The speaker is trying to forestall one possible reading (the story with the selfish theme) in favor of another one (the story with the theme of caring for children). There are, nevertheless, two stories at work here, both exerting an influence on what happens. The practices of active listening tend to invite mediators to select one story for reflection and paraphrase, but more sophisticated listening invites us to listen and respond to both stories.

Usually, in an established or entrenched conflict, one story has become dominant and has narrowed the narrative focus so that this account is the one accorded principle attention by the storyteller. But careful listening can always discern the presence of other stories hidden in the midst of what a person tells. Michael White developed a name for this kind of listening. He called it *double listening* (2007). Double listening means listening at the same time for expressions of the conflict story and for elements of other stories, particularly for those elements that might become part of a possible counter-story. It involves listening for both the story that has become dominant and for other possible stories that sit alongside, or behind, or underneath the dominant story. It also involves listening for the points of bifurcation (a term used often by Barnett Pearce, 2007, p. 96) where different stories part company.

We want to advocate here not just process-oriented active listening, but also content-oriented listening to just what story is being selected out for emphasis and what other stories are being relegated to the background. The assumption of double listening is that recuperating overlooked stories can often make the story from which a person is operating less fixed, more complex, richer, more negotiable, and more open to another's perspective.

Let us now outline a series of practical ways in which a focus on double listening can help a mediator to attend to the stories that might otherwise lay masked or subjugated. Each of these suggestions for what to listen for involve attending to little ironies, bifurcation points, unique outcomes (White, & Epston's, 1990, term, after Erving Goffman), momentary asides, story elements that are glossed over, actions that contradict the escalation of the conflict, and so on.

DOUBLE LISTENING TO PEOPLE'S PRESENCE IN THE ROOM

The first aspect of a *counter story* (Nelson, 2001) to the escalation of a conflict lies in the parties' very presence in the room, before they have even opened their mouths. Why did they decide to show up? There can be various reasons, but usually at least one reason lies in a sense of hope that something can be sorted out with the other party. Rather than always beginning a mediation process by defining the problem, it is possible to ask people to articulate this sense of hope.

> *My guess is that, when you came here today, you had some sense of hope about what kind of conversation we might have and what it might lead to. I wonder whether you could start by speaking to that?*

Notice that we are not asking people to center their speaking in what they want, or in their underlying 'interests' (although some may answer in this way). Asking for people's hopes involves eliciting something bigger than personal desires. It calls forth a person's best self and her most generous and inclusive voice. Someone might respond by saying something like, 'My hope is that we can have a civil conversation about our children. I am sick of just arguing about them. We need to talk things through before it gets worse and we need your help to do this. '

Note the reference to an escalating conflict story that is getting worse and, on the other hand, the desire for a different relational story that is about 'talking things through'. The counter story is even given a name—'civil conversation'. From the point of view of this counter story, the speaker is 'sick of just arguing'. Presumably, within the conflict story, arguing would be understood as just what is. It would be surrounded by an aura of inevitability. Double listening requires us to hear two stories here. We can surely explore what the arguments are about but it might also be important to dwell for a moment on the exploration of the counter story.

Mediator: *I am interested in your hope for something different, for a civil conversation, for talking it through. Help me understand why is that important for you?*

1st Party: *Well. It's important for the children that they don't just see us fighting. They've seen enough of that and it has been affecting them. They are both showing signs of insecurity and we need to work together to make things as stable as possible for them.*

Mediator (to the other party): *Is that important to you as well or do you have some other hopes for what we might do here today?*

2nd party: *I don't want the children to suffer either. Of course I don't! I came here hoping we could sort out some arrangements so we didn't have to slug it out in court. It's so demeaning and also so expensive. We can do better than that.*

Mediator: *What would 'doing better than that' look like from your point of view?*

2nd party: *It would mean being honest with each other, sticking to what is best for the children and not treating them as objects to have a tug of war over and being fair and generous with each other.*

After such an exchange, the mediator has a sense of both the problem story that involves arguing, fighting, and a tug-of-war over the children, and a possible counter story that involves talking things through, holding a civil conversation, sorting out arrangements, and being fair and generous. If, over the next hour, the conversation slips into an escalation of the 'arguing' story, the mediator can ask the two parties:

So does what you are saying now resemble more the fighting you said you were hoping to step out of or the civil conversation you were hoping to achieve? Which would you prefer?

DOUBLE LISTENING TO TWO STORIES WITHIN THE SAME SENTENCE

We have been talking about double listening to what people communicate simply by their presence in the room and growing a conversation about hope from the meaning of their presence. Now we shall focus on further verbal expressions that contain references to more than one story. Very often double listening opens up the complexity present in a single sentence. One way to start to notice this is to listen for the word 'but' in the middle of a sentence. It regularly serves as a hinge around which two stories can swing. Here is an example, 'If we could just make the transition from married partners to parents we could still discuss Sam's future, but we need to discuss what is in Sam's best interests and not have the personal issues get in the way.'

Two possible scenarios are present in this utterance—one in which the personal issues get in the way, and one in which the transition to collaborating parents is successfully negotiated. Double listening hears and responds to both stories and can allow a mediator to elaborate and contrast both of them.

Here is another example of a statement that requires double listening, 'Sometimes I have a little bit of trouble accepting that he wants to work with me as a parent, because of the things that have happened between us.'

Double listening suggests two stories here—one of the desire to accept her ex-partner's willingness to work collaboratively, and one in which this is 'difficult to accept'. Neither story is, in itself, more true than the other. Both might be made true by the decision to perform acts of living on the basis of the story. A further example follows.

'We have had our own disagreements. It obviously didn't work out and we can't fix the differences. But we have also seen other families that have gone through divorce, and the effect on their children is not something our daughter needs to experience in her life.'

The word 'but' appears in the middle of this utterance. It is often an indicator of two stories on either side of it. On one side is the story of differences that led to frustration and cannot be resolved. On the other side is the story of a desire not to let the divorce cause pain to their children. There is no need to integrate the two stories. They both exist and at different moments might be expected to exert a pull on the speaker's actions. It is better to appreciate them as competing stories, each with some force behind it, and to invite the parties to think about the ethical decision of which story most deserves to be nurtured and grown.

DOUBLE LISTENING TO THE EXPRESSION OF EMOTIONS

Active listening often assumes that emotional expression is singular and definitive of what is in the heart of a speaker, but double listening lets us hear the situation as much more complex. If we start from the assumption that an emotional experience is not just an event in the heart of an individual but an aspect of a relational exchange (the social constructionist position), then a range of possibilities come into view. For example, an emotion might be considered not just as an internal physiological event but also as a performance before others with an intended effect. Any intention to influence others in this way might be considered a practice of power. In Foucault's (1982) terms, it is an *action upon others' actions* (p. 220). It might also be considered a response to a situation in the world around and, perhaps, as a judgment on a contextual event. If I am angry, then I am not happy with what has been happening and judge it to be wrong. I also implicitly want it to change and have at least some idea of what else I would prefer. If I am sad, then I might be expressing my affection for what no longer pertains. I am expressing, on the one hand, a sense of missing and, on the other, an implicit positive valuing of what once was. If I am afraid, then I am concerned about a possible eventuation that will not be pleasant and, at the same time, a preference for what might feel safer.

Michael White's notion (after Derrida) of the *absent but implicit* (White, 2000, p. 153) is useful here. It helps us to ask, for example, with regard to something I am angry about, what it might be like to turn the coin over. The story that I am not happy about something that exists is one version of events. If we flip this story over, there is always something else that I would prefer to what I am frustrated by. Double listening allows us to inquire into both the source of the anger (*What are you not happy with?*) and to flip it over and inquire into the absent but implicit (*And what would you prefer?*). If the emotion is one of sadness, double listening also allows us to flip the story over. If I am sad about the loss or absence of something, then the flipside is a story about the affection I used to hold for its presence. There is now potential for this affection to be actively remembered (as in *re-membering conversations*, White, 2007; Hedtke, & Winslade, 2004) or reconstituted in some way. If the emotion is one of fear, then there might be an absent but implicit preference for some actions that can contribute to safety. If a person is feeling despair, then there is always an implicit story of hope that has been lost and might perhaps be recuperated. In other words, there is always some other side to the coin. Flipping the coin over produces a different story. Double listening allows us to hear both the emotion that is present and the one that is absent but implicit.

EXCEPTIONS TO A DOMINANT STORY

Double listening also alerts mediators to the presence of exceptions to the dominance of a conflict story. Such exceptions may exist in a number of places, if we train ourselves to be alert to them. For example, people often find conflict painful and create pathways of escape (*lines of flight*, in Deleuze, 1995). They stop fighting and withdraw. They refuse to allow matters to escalate further. They establish a truce. They implicitly agree to skirt around the touchy issues. They opt for little breaks of calmness in between conflictual exchanges. These are potentially not just gaps in a conflict narrative but also openings to a different narrative. We might inquire into their significance.

How come it was important to you to not allow things to escalate further?

Does it suggest how you would like to change the direction of where things have been heading?

Does it indicate what you value and don't want to see damaged any further?

There can also be small moments of cooperation that continue to manifest themselves in the shadow of conflict. Parents who are in conflict over arrangements for the care of their children might have a phone call that was civil or a pick-up and drop-off that went smoothly. Such moments of cooperation might also be found in people's willingness to work together in domains of living other than those that are conflicted.

So in the middle of intense arguments you were able to set things aside and concentrate on ensuring that your daughter had a memorable birthday. How did you manage that?

Exceptions to the dominance of a conflict narrative can also be found in the expression of overtures for peaceful resolution. These can be offered in the middle of a mediation, or in gestures of generosity at some other time. Here is an example.

'Look, I'm willing to accept that the old agreement is no longer going to work. Within myself, I have come to that place, with some reservations still. But anyway, now I'm willing to start to work on something new, some new basis for going forward.'

The speaker is offering a withdrawal of commitment to an aspect of the conflict story. Double listening hears the pull of the old story in the allusion to a sense of reservation. The statement also amounts to a significant move into a new story. A mediator might capitalize on it by first clarifying it and then by asking the other party to make meaning of it.

Mediator*: So what difference does it make to hear him say that?*

Party B: *It's positive ... although I am not sure how much I can trust it.*

Mediator: *So you have reservations too. But, despite those, you hear what he said as positive?*

Party B: *Yes.*

Mediator: *So if what he says could be trusted, what might you be able to offer in return?*

Party B: *I can begin to work on a new plan too.*

Double listening enables the conflict story to be acknowledged. At the same time, it invites the development of a counter story that encourages willingness to generate a new plan. The mediator often has to assist the opening of a fragile possible counter story by shielding it, as happens here, from being squashed by the power of the dominant conflict story.

Sometimes double listening can involve hearing the difference between a story that is stalled at the point of an intention and a more dominant story that has been acted upon. Here is an example.

'I have been feeling bad about what I said last week and I have been trying to get up the courage to apologize. But the arguments just keep getting in the way of doing that.'

From the narrative perspective, there is nothing more true or more real about the way that 'the arguments' are preventing the intention to apologize from becoming manifest. It is just a case of one narrative overshadowing another one. Recognizing this, a narrative mediator practicing double listening might seek to open up a line of narrative from the stalled intention.

So the arguments keep interfering with your intention to apologize. But if that interference were not happening, what sort of apology might you want to offer?

Sometimes too the practice of double listening can mean granting space to the voice of an actual other person. This voice might be expressed in the words of someone influential in the speaker's life or it might be a virtual voice. This is in line with Deleuze and Guattari's (1994) claim that what is *virtual* is no less real (in its effects) than an *actual* voice. A virtual voice can exert a powerful real force that double listening hears as an opening to a different narrative. Here is an example from a conflict coaching conversation. (Conflict coaching may be an alternative to mediation when one party to a conflict cannot be present.) Adriana is speaking about a telephone conflict with the agency from which she rents her home. As she talks on the phone she is holding her baby in her arms.

Adriana: *I was very angry with how this person was speaking to me, but I was also aware that I had my daughter in my arms and I didn't want to upset her.*

Mediator: *You didn't want to frighten your daughter? What message did you want your daughter to receive in this context?*

Adriana: *I was concerned about how she might be affected by hearing me get angry. I didn't want her to feel the brunt of my anger at someone else. She wouldn't necessarily be able to distinguish that I was not upset with her.*

Mediator: *Did I understand correctly that you were relating to the person from the property management office and being a parent at the same time?*

Adriana: *Yes, I was torn in two directions at that moment.*

Mediator: *If we could imagine that in the future your daughter might be able to speak to what she was learning from you in this moment, what might she say?*

Adriana: *That I was supporting her. That I was upset with someone else, but I was protecting her from being affected by it.*

Mediator: *As you reflect on what happened, how would you*

describe how you handled yourself as a result in the phone call?

Adriana: *It wasn't as bad as I thought it was going to be. I was relatively pleased with how I handled myself. I stayed calm and respectful and I stood my ground and I got him to listen to me.*

Mediator: *So would it be fair to say that your daughter's voice, even though it was an imagined voice in your head, helped you to respond to the caller in a way that you feel pleased about and to avoid getting angry in a way you would have afterwards felt not so happy with?*

Adriana: *Yes that's right, when I think about it.*

It is often useful in double listening to characterize the two narratives as competing voices in a person's head. Being 'torn in two directions' is not treated as a pathology, nor as an obstacle to the expression of true feelings, but as another resource to be drawn upon. Multiple stories give us choices and, in this instance, enable Adriana to make a choice of response in a conflict situation that she feels happy with. To honor this possibility, it is necessary for the conflict coach to be double listening. What is produced for Adriana is a sense of agency in this situation, rather than a sense of being a victim with few choices but to suffer.

Understanding the principle of double listening is often experienced as introducing a tone of lightness into a tense situation. It does not have to involve seeing the silver lining, or accentuating the positive, or jollying people along. Just noticing the alternative narrative and inviting people to establish a preference can be enough. You do not even have to give up on the conflict story. Just acknowledging the existence of another possible account can be sufficient.

SUMMARY FOCUS

- In the end, double listening is a practice founded on a process of differentiation, rather than on integration. It values complexity ahead of linear certitude.

- Double listening treats the existence of multiple narratives as a rich resource, rather than as a complication to be simplified away.

- Double listening encourages mediators to listen for points of bifurcation in the middle of a narrative, or even of a sentence. A bifurcation is like a fork in the road and there are always many of them in the telling of any narrative.

- Double listening hears even intense emotional expressions as potentially giving way to subtle distinctions, if we turn the coin over and look at the obverse side.

- Double listening alerts us to listen for the existence of alternative narratives sitting alongside those narratives that escalate the conflict.

- To notice that there are two or more possible stories allows people to make shifts from one to the other. Everything in the conflict story does not even need to be resolved for this shift to be negotiated.

- Double listening represents an advance on the well-known practice of active listening that carries the danger of locking people into a single story. The practices of paraphrasing and reflecting are not rendered irrelevant but are put to a new use.

- The new use is defined by a difference in what we listen for, rather than just in how we might listen.

CHAPTER 4
EXTERNALIZING AND MAPPING THE EFFECTS

'SO DOES THAT WAY OF talking work for you both?' asked a mediator, taking care not to sound sarcastic or patronizing.

There was a pause in which both parties appeared non-plussed and were uncertain how to respond. Juan and Bernice were colleagues in a workplace who had become embroiled in a dispute and were arguing loudly. The question took them out of the detail of an argument and invited them to soar above their own conversation.

In the pause, the mediator continued, 'I'm just curious, you see, whether that way of talking is getting you any closer to the kind of "teamwork" that you both agreed you wanted to re-establish? Is it allowing you to go in that direction or not?'

With a little shamefaced embarrassment, both parties agreed that they were not getting anywhere by shouting and blaming each other.

'Does it suit you both as individuals then? Like, is it part of your preferred style of relationship?' the mediator continued.

This time there was slightly quicker agreement that it did not fit with their hopes or intentions.

'So I am wondering two things,' said the mediator. 'The first is how that way of talking took over from what seems for both of you to be your better judgment? How did you let it do that to you?'

Silence.

'And the second thing I wonder,' the mediator eventually proceeded, 'is what effect it is having? It sounds like that way of talking gets you both heated and your voices start to rise. What would you say it is doing to both of you?'

It took a little bit of coaxing and asking the same question several different ways, but eventually Bernice and Juan, were able to acknowledge what 'that way of talking' was doing to them.

'I hate it,' said Bernice. 'It makes me nervous of Juan and I start to get a headache and I just can't concentrate on getting any work done.'

'I feel embarrassed that you have seen me getting down to that level,' said Juan. 'In fact, I feel embarrassed anyway that we are in this situation. It's like I'm a leper around the office. Everyone tries to keep their distance at the moment.'

'So what would each of you prefer, other than the shouting and blaming?'

This question was easier to answer.

'I would like us to have a calmer conversation, actually,'

said Juan. 'One in which we can talk about what we need to figure out in order to be able to work together.'

The mediator was ready with another question.

'So how would a calmer conversation be different from that way of talking?'

'I guess it would involve sorting out what the differences have been and trying to reach better understanding between us about those things,' said Juan.

Bernice had been listening pensively.

The mediator prompted her, 'So what do you make of what Juan just said?'

She was hesitant.

'I basically agree with what he said ... but I don't know if I can trust him not to start coming across all macho and aggressive like that again.'

The mediator summarized.

'So you agree with the idea of a calmer conversation. It's just that that way of talking, the aggression and the macho included, have made it harder for you to have any trust in him right now.'

Bernice nodded cautiously.

'And Juan, you would prefer not to have that way of talking continue to rule your relationship and demand that you do its bidding. In fact your personal preference is for calmer conversation. Have I got that right?'

They both nodded slowly, agreeing for the third time in a row.

This exchange does not, of course, address all of the outstanding issues and there is still a long way to go before they have established 'teamwork'. But it begins the process, typical of narrative mediation, of inviting parties to step out of a conflict story and to open up a counter story. We shall recap elements of this shift and point out the purpose of the mediator's responses.

Most of what the mediator says takes the form of questions. The mediator deliberately does not tell Juan or Bernice what to do because this might lead to more defensive responses. The questions asked are not so much about the content of the parties' stories as about their relationship with those stories. We picked up the story after a conversation about the details of the problematic conflict and about each person's perspectives on that conflict. From there, things had deteriorated into name-calling and exchanges of blame and the atmosphere had slipped into what was close to a shouting match. This interaction was interrupted by the mediator because, from our perspective, there is little to be gained by encouraging the venting of strong emotions in such a situation. We do not believe in the usefulness or therapeutic value of the cathartic release of emotion. If anything, the performance of angry blaming is likely to make it harder for Bernice and Juan to realize their hopes for better teamwork.

EXTERNALIZING

The mediator's initial intervention is therefore a calculated attempt to invite the parties to step out of the argument. She does so by initiating an *externalizing conversation* (White, & Epston, 1990; Morgan, 2000). This involves giving the problem story a name - in this case it is called, temporarily at least, 'that way of talking.' This expression is used repeatedly by the mediator and it is spoken of consistently as separate from the two parties. It is the problem and they are almost the victims of its actions. If any blame is to be assigned, it is 'that way of talking' that must wear it, rather than Juan or Bernice. It has had designs on them, persuaded them to its way of thinking, sometimes whispered convincing lies in their ears, enacted through them gendered behavioral patterns of 'macho' aggression and female anxiety, and interfered with their better judgment.

The linguistic shift involved, if sustained, starts to exert an effect on the grammar of the relationship between the two parties. As typically happens, Bernice and Juan start to join with this form of language, almost without noticing it. This way of speaking objectifies the problem and linguistically starts to line the parties up alongside each other. In the exchange above, it is noticeable that Bernice and Juan have been arguing heatedly but, when the mediator starts using externalizing language, they actually agree on several things quite easily.

Externalizing conversation, however, is more than a linguistic gimmick. It involves the enactment of a principle. The best expression of this principle is Michael White's aphorism which has become emblematic for narrative practice, *The person is not the problem; the problem is the problem* (1989, p. 6). Aside from the effort to avoid nonproductive blaming, the principle at stake is the social constructionist one that we are the products of ways of speaking in conversation, or discourse, rather than products of our essential nature. If we, therefore, change the way in which we speak about a situation, we potentially change our experience of it.

A caution worth noting about externalizing language is that it matters what the problem is called. It would have the potential to backfire if it only referred to one party's perspective on the conflict. Ideally, it should include reference to what both parties experience as problematic, but often there is a yawning gap between the diverse accounts they each represent. There are various options for externalizing in this context. A mediator can refer to the whole situation. In the case above, 'that way of talking' includes both parties' verbal expressions. Sometimes, however, one person may be shouting and the other may be silent and refusing to talk. In such a circumstance the mediator may need to externalize both approaches separately and link them together as, for example, the 'aggression-avoidance scenario'. Yet another option for externalizing is to trace the series of exchanges of a conflict as they have developed into a vicious downward spiral of events and then to label the whole cycle of events as the problem, obviating the search for who started it all. The downward spiral itself can then be externalized as the problem and questions can be asked about the parties' relationship with it.

Sometimes the externalized name for the problematic conflict spontaneously emerges in the conversation. Someone will exclaim, 'This is just a mess!' The mediator is then able to pick up on the word 'mess' and inquire into its shaping of the parties' relationship, rather than into their creation of the mess.

'So how is this "mess" taking over your better intentions?'

On other occasions, more work is required to name it. The best strategy is then to ask the disputing parties to come up with a name. The mediator might ask:

'If we were to think of a name to describe this problem that we are up against, which seems to have been causing you both so much pain, what might we call it? Can you suggest a name for this whole thing?'

Notice how this question positions people to respond. It (a third party) is constructed as the problem, rather than them (first and second party). They are positioned alongside each other as partners sharing in a joint struggle against it. The shift in positioning is subtle, but potentially makes for a significant difference in how two people who have been sharply at odds are now joined in relationship with the conflict.

MAPPING THE EFFECTS OF THE PROBLEM

The next challenge is to capitalize on the momentum of the externalizing conversation that has just begun. The danger is that 'that way of talking' will quickly return, unless the parties decide to move further away from it. After all, 'that way of talking' is an element in a relational story that has been dominating 'teamwork' and squeezing it, and other possibilities, out of the picture. Developing a conversation about the effects of the conflict serves the purpose of creating further distance from the problem that has been dogging the relationship between the parties.

In the example above, the mediator asks the disputing people to specify what 'it is doing to you both'. It is common for people to speak first about the effects of a problem like this in emotional terms. It might be described as 'upsetting', as making them 'angry', or 'afraid' of what the other person might do. Rather than treating such emotional expressions as communicative goals to be recognized or acknowledged, a narrative mediator might treat them as entry points to a story. Curiosity will soon lead to a story that is richer than a single emotional expression and contains actions and thoughts and feelings all working together.

There is another consideration here too. Mediation is not therapy (although it may often have therapeutic effects) and mediators should take care not to engineer a conversation in which parties to a dispute are unwittingly persuaded into opening up a seam of vulnerability in front of someone who might use this as a weapon to hurt them with, should the conflict continue to fester. We, therefore, prefer not to actively inquire too far into a party's inner experience of the effects of a conflict in front of the other party. On the other hand, people are often happy to divulge elements of such experience and can feel some relief from the effects of the conflict narrative, if they know that they both share some sense of distress.

There are plenty of other domains in which the effects of a conflict might be registered and which can be inquired about. It is not uncommon for people to report distress in terms of physiological effects: headaches, difficulty sleeping, muscle tension, nausea, and so on. In a family dispute, family relationships can be disrupted or irritations between family members magnified. In an organizational dispute, the genre in which the effects of a conflict might be spoken about can be quite different from a family conflict. For example, a workplace conflict might have effects on people's ability to perform their job functions. Lowered staff morale might be noticed among colleagues. Customers might decrease and profits become affected. Colleagues may come to dread meetings in which they are obliged to interact with each other. Or people may spend inordinate amounts of time thinking about, talking about, or obsessing about, a conflicted relationship, at the expense of other activities they would prefer to engage in.

Mapping the effects of a conflict can also take account of the development of a narrative through time by inquiring into the past, present and future. Effects can be noticed to have happened already in the past, sometimes proving difficult to reverse. They can also sometimes be noticed in the immediate present, even affecting what is happening in the mediation itself. There is an example of this in the story above when the mediator recognizes Bernice's caution about trusting what Juan is saying. Effects of a conflict can also be tracked into an imagined future. Mediator questions such as the following help achieve this.

> *'It sounds like this "mess" is already wreaking a fair bit of havoc for you both. But what if it were to continue unchecked? What if it were to get worse? What would that be like and how would you manage it?'*

Mediation participants often shudder at the thought that things could get worse and are often even more inclined to move toward a change.

In the last chapter we dwelt on the value of double listening. This practice can continue while developing an externalizing conversation and mapping the effects of a conflict. Such conversations help people to dis-identify with a conflict narrative, to at least a small extent. In the process, a gap can open up in which what they would prefer can be considered. Here are some examples of questions a mediator might ask to accomplish both mapping the effects of a conflict narrative and contrasting it with something else.

- *Has this conflict got you acting out of character? What would be more in character for you?*

- *How has the tension led you to say things or do things against your better judgment? What would your better judgment lead you to say or do?*

- *What has this argument deprived you of?*

- *Are there any intentions either of you has harbored to make things better between you that have been squashed by the interference of this struggle?*

If there is opportunity, the exploration of the effects of a conflict can go on for some time. Immediate effects will surface readily but, if a mediator is willing to pursue the inquiry, less obvious but nonetheless important effects can be surfaced. Many of these will have been scarcely noticeable before this point but noticing them can have a salutary effect on the parties' motivation for change. A mediator needs to be patient and give time for less obvious effects to be surfaced and at the same time remain persistent in the inquiry. A simple question can serve this purpose. Here it is: *'What else?'*

It can be useful to ask this question in five different ways, but essentially the message is the same: reach a little further and think a little harder and see what emerges. Time taken to do this is often well spent.

FURTHER EXAMPLES

Inclusion of some further examples of the practice of externalizing and mapping the effects helps explain the value of such conversation. Here are some examples of this practice in action.

DIVORCING COUPLE

In a mediation with a couple who were close to deciding to divorce, one of them spoke of the relationship in terms of 'alienation', 'lack of openness', 'lack of closeness' and the other person spoke about 'financial worry' and 'the unemployment situation'. Rather than seeking to force these different points of focus together, it made more sense to develop two parallel externalizing conversations.

The mediator also did not attempt to inquire into the causes of the perceived lack of closeness or alienation or indeed into the sources of the financial worry or the unemployment situation. The couple was forthcoming anyway with stories that explained the role of these problems in their relationship. To inquire into the causes of these problems was unlikely to open up space for a counter story. The speculative theorizing that might result can tend to lend weight to the inevitability of a conflict. It is more productive to inquire into the effects of these problems, because it is the effects which can more easily be operated on to bring about change. Lines of force can often be bent to enable a shift in direction.

The mediator therefore inquired of one party into the effects of 'alienation' and 'lack of closeness', treating them as lines of force that were producing a relational identity, rather than as aspects of the essence of the person. The mediator heard how these externalized problems were leading to a sense of 'tension' and 'frustration', sometimes 'resentment' and an experience of passing like 'two ships in the night'.

After a few minutes, the mediator switched to the other party and inquired into the effects of the 'financial worry' and the 'unemployment situation' on the parties in conflict. The mediator heard about 'unproductive time' and 'squandered days' and of how the situation 'robbed us of intimacy' and was leading to a sense of 'despair' and an inclination to 'give up'. The two conversations came together when an agreement was offered that they both shared the experience of passing like 'two ships in the night'.

DISPUTING SISTERS

Another example features a dispute between two sisters, Brenda and Gina, over their mother's will. After exploring a number of relationship issues and mapping the effects of these on each person individually, the mediator turns to asking about the effects of the conflict on their relationship.

'What impact would you say this whole thing [a simple externalization] has had on the relationship between you?'

Brenda is the first to answer. She picks up on the externalizing language and uses it herself.

'It has distanced us. It has felt like bitterness between us.'

Gina adds, 'And the mistrust. Because, of course, I was investigating to see who helped my mom revise the will. So there was mistrust.'

Even as she says this, the externalizing language helps her take a small step away from the mistrust. The mediator helps this along.

'So it increased your sense of suspicion?'

'Definitely,' says Gina.

'And would that fit with how you normally think of yourself—to be suspicious of your sister?'

'No,' says Gina emphatically. 'She's my sister. I would never question her. But this is a big thing. And I know that our father had helped mom create the will, so I didn't know why she decided to change it in the last six months.'

'And I don't know either,' Brenda inserts quickly. 'I didn't have a part in that.'

In the next chapter we shall illustrate how the mediator opens up a counter story of Brenda and Gina's relationship. For now it is enough to notice how the relationship between them is characterized in externalizing language. Its effects on their relationship are mapped, as well as the effects on them both as individuals.

WHERE DOES THIS GET US?

Where does the development of an externalizing conversation and a careful mapping of the effects leave us? If done well, it can lead a conversation to the edge of commitment to a different relationship story. Amassing all of the effects of a conflict together can be experienced as illuminating. Sometimes for the first time, people begin to see a comprehensive overview of the work that a conflict has been doing. A mediator can even ask participants to reflect on this opportunity.

'What is it like to notice all of the effects that this conflict has been having?'

Responses vary, of course, to such a question but it is not uncommon to hear people say something like the following.

'It's quite ridiculous when I think about it!'

'It's got to stop!'

'We can't go on like this. Something's got to change!'

It is also not uncommon for both parties to be in agreement on this point. From here, it is easy for a mediator to ask, 'So what would you prefer?'

In the response to this question, people begin to open up a counter story. The development of this counter story is the subject of the next chapter.

SUMMARY FOCUS

- Conflict stories often feature blame and objectification of the other.

- Externalizing conversations turn the tables so that the problem is objectified and blamed rather than the person.

- Externalizing repositions disputing parties so that they are lined up alongside each other against the problem, rather than against each other.

- Externalizing is more than a linguistic gimmick. It places problems back in the discourse, rather than in the nature of persons.

- Mapping the effects of a problem is a useful way to extend the effects of an externalization.

- It is more productive to explore the effects of a conflict than the causes of it. Effects can be altered, whereas speculating about causes can make it all seem too inevitable and overly determined.

- Effects of the problem may be traced in emotional, physiological, relational, social, and financial domains.

- Once you have heard about some of the effects of a problem, ask, 'What else?' so that less obvious but nonetheless important effects will not be overlooked.

- Noticing the extent of the effects of a conflict can increase the motivation to embrace a counter story.

CHAPTER 5
BUILDING COUNTER STORIES

'GINA, YOU MENTIONED THAT THE conflict about your mother's will created distance between you and your sister and has fueled feelings of bitterness and mistrust. You also said you don't like to be this suspicious of your sister and you hope that the effects of the conflict would stop. Can you tell me some more about what would you prefer instead?'

'I would say ... validation of feelings. That's a big thing.'

'So a relationship in which feelings were validated.'

'Yes,' Gina agreed.

This mediation is at the point where a story of a conflict has been explored and its effects on the parties noted. Gina and Brenda are willing to reject this story in favor of something else, but the something else is still vague and needs to be elaborated. The mediator is asking questions to bring forward a possible counter story, one that features the parties' preferences for how the relationship between them might become. The details of any agreement for change are delayed in narrative mediation until after the preferred story of relationship has been articulated.

'So what kind of relationship would do that?' asks the mediator, seeking from Gina a description of the relationship story.

A general description of the relationship story is beyond where Gina has yet reached, so she resorts to the fleshing out of relevant details.

'I know she said that she's part of my son's life, which she is, on occasion.' Gina then turns to Brenda, 'But it would be nice if you would spend more time with our family.'

The mediator notes down this idea, 'So it would include spending more time with your family. Anything else?'

Gina thinks and then offers, 'Maybe not suggesting that my lifestyle is all that bad, as far as my choice of being a parent.' She turns to Brenda again, 'It seems as if you're standoffish about my lifestyle and my choices.'

The mediator acknowledges Gina's statements and links it back to what she said a moment earlier, 'This is an area where you'd like some validation of your choices in life as being worthwhile?'

'Maybe tell me that I'm a good mom. That's something I've worked hard for.'

Generating a different relationship story is not quite the same thing as generating a different relationship. Narrative mediation, however, works on the assumption that a shift to having a different story governing the relationship will lead toward the details of relational events lining up with that governing story. This story may take on a multitude of possible names. In this case, the immediately available names, arising out of the parties' own language, were a story of 'acting like sisters' (Brenda's earlier description) or a story of 'validation' (Gina's name).

Here we illustrate the process of generating a departure from the conflict story through growing Gina's story of 'validation'. Gina began with a complaint about the validation that was not there, but it contained within it an implicit preference for something better. Recognizing it as an opening to a viable relationship possibility, the mediator asks questions about this small opening to a different story. It is an example of a *unique outcome* (White, & Epston, 1990; White, 2007; Winslade, & Monk, 2000).

A unique outcome is understood in narrative practice as an instance (an event, an utterance, a desire, or an intention) of something that lies outside of the conflict story. It does not fit with the conflictual account of relationship that has dominated the meaning the parties have been making. Often it might lie neglected, on its own in the wilderness, without companions, starved of meaning and thirsty for recognition. Without attention, it may die for lack of significance.

A new story, however, has to start somewhere and a unique outcome may also be a potential starting place for a different account of a relationship. In order for this to happen, a mediator needs to ask questions that fill it out into a full-blown story, rather than an isolated moment. Isolated moments are too easily swamped by powerful dominant stories and rendered impotent, but they can also be strengthened by linking them together and allocating meaning to them. Then further instances of such meaning may be elaborated and a story can grow. If protected from the ravages of the conflict, this story can eventually rival the conflict story and serve as a viable choice that disputing parties might opt for. Let us pick up the conversation with Gina and Brenda again to observe this development.

Gina says, 'I wish we could establish mutual understanding. You want me to validate your photography business. I want you to validate my parenting. Maybe we can better understand each other.'

There is a possibility here, but at the moment it is an abstracted idea and needs fleshing out on what Michael White (2007; after Jerome Bruner, 1986) refers to as the *landscape of action.* The landscape of action is the territory where the plot of a relationship story takes place. The mediator seeks to expand into this landscape.

'Tell me about the history of these things. I would like to hear about any situation in which you experienced some validation?'

'I can't really remember any time where that happened.'

Gina's reply is a typical first response to such a question. The mediator hears it not so much as an indication that such moments of validation did not take place. Instead it is interpreted as an indication of how the dominance of the conflict story can make moments of contradiction invisible. He persists.

'Well, what would be the thing that would come closest to that?'

Gina still cannot see past the conflict story, 'I'd have to get back to you on that.'

Still persisting, the mediator asks the question in another way, 'I guess what I'm asking is, in the history of your relationship, has there been a single instance of something Brenda did that you experienced as validating?'

It stands to reason that in most relationships between sisters such moments must exist, even if they are hard to identify when people are embroiled in conflict.

Gina thinks harder and this time comes back with a tentative response. 'Maybe when Brenda comes over and visits our family. There's been a better spirit.'

The unique outcome is fragile and needs acknowledgement.

'Okay,' responds the mediator slowly. 'So there have been times when you've had those visits that have felt like a better spirit.'

Gina's response is slightly less tentative, 'Yeah. She was able to have fun and it felt like everything fit perfectly.'

The mediator seeks to tie the description down to the precise detail of a particular moment in time.

'Are you thinking of a particular occasion as you say this?'

Gina did have a particular memory.

'It was a Wednesday, when we have taco night. She came over and just hung out and we watched television.'

The mediator attempts to gauge the significance of this occasion, 'So it wasn't a big deal. It was just a Wednesday taco night watching television. But that felt neat to you, somehow.'

'It did,' mused Gina. 'It felt like what we were supposed to do all along.'

It transpires, however, that this event took place a while ago, before their mother became ill, and may be, therefore, less significant than if it were more recent. The mediator, therefore, continues the search for more recent examples.

'Can I ask then whether there are any other little instances like that one, that would fit with greater understanding and validation between you?'

Now Gina finds such moments easier to identify.

'I guess she did validate me when I took charge of the funeral arrangements. There was a moment when we sat alone, before we talked about the will. We cried together and were able to talk about a lot of things. It just felt like we were appreciative of each other.'

Brenda voices agreement.

'So for you, Brenda, was that a moment that was closer to "acting like sisters"?'

'Yeah.'

'And you were able to have family connection in that moment?'

Gina responds, 'She was very grateful and I think she commented on how beautiful the funeral was and said thank you for taking over.'

The mediator seeks to extract more significance from this moment.

'What was that like for you, Brenda, that she did all the organizing?'

'She does do a lot of those kinds of things and I don't ever tell her they're appreciated. I do appreciate that she does that stuff and is like the glue of the family ... I haven't ever said that before.'

Gina is moved, 'Thank you. That was nice. The glue! That's sweet!'

Wanting to hold this moment aloft, the mediator asks, 'What did you like about her saying that?'

'All along,' say Gina, 'that's the validation I wanted.'

This exchange between them is like a unique outcome that takes place in the immediate present. It is clear now that there is another relationship story they can share, other than the one dominated by conflict. It may need to be developed further and a mediator would need to exercise careful judgment on this score. The issues around their mother's will are still outstanding and now need to be engaged. However, the parties are now situated in a relational story of 'understanding' and 'validation' from where they can negotiate their differences productively. The conflict story has not disappeared, but there is now a viable counter story. The spirit of this counter story can now be invoked to aid them in sorting through what they need to negotiate.

How was this counter story accessed? It began from an inquiry into what they were not happy with and the tracing of the effects of the conflict on each of them. Implicit within any statement of what a person is not happy about is the opposite - what she would prefer. Narrative practice constructs these opposites as competing stories. The mediator here has listened to both stories. Gradually, the inquiry has turned to the preferred story of relationship. Plot events in this story have been found. Thematic elements have been identified and different characterizations have been elaborated. The story has been fleshed out enough to be recognized by the parties as what they value.

A COUNTER STORY IN A RESTORATIVE CONFERENCE

In this section we shall offer an example of growing a different story of relationship that comes from a *restorative conference* in a school setting. Fuller details of the process for a narrative conferencing process can be found elsewhere (Winslade, & Williams, 2012; Winslade, & Monk, 2008; Restorative Practices Development Team, 2004). Here we shall concentrate particularly on the process of growing a counter story.

A conference has been called to address an incident in which Aaron assaulted Theo on the grounds of a middle school as both were leaving for home. Aaron was much bigger than Theo and knocked him to the ground with a punch to the head and then proceeded to kick him in the stomach several times. The school treated the incident as a serious assault and Aaron was suspended for three days. During this time a restorative conference was set up to determine whether Aaron would be willing to change his behavior. If not, the principal was ready to recommend to the school board that he be expelled.

Attending the conference with Aaron were his mother, Tina, and grandmother, Florence. Theo was there along with his father, Albert, and mother, Angelica. Also present were Aaron's English teacher, Mike, and his social worker, Laura.

The meeting went through a process of establishing details of the offense and underlining its seriousness. Aaron did not dispute the school's account of what had happened and had indicated ahead of the meeting his willingness to make amends for what he had done.

Then the conference facilitator drew a circle on a whiteboard underneath the words, 'The person is not the problem; the problem is the problem,' and asked each person present to name the problem from their own perspective. Each description of the problem was listed in externalizing language in the middle of the circle. The list included the following words: 'vicious assault'; 'an aggression problem'; 'gang-like violence'; 'lack of verbal skills'; 'negative attitude'; 'bullying' and 'stand-over tactics'. Even Aaron called it 'fighting'.

Looking at the list the facilitator said, 'So all of these names are the problem. Now I want to ask each of you in turn to speak about one effect of this problem [pointing to the list on the whiteboard] on you personally. Theo, you were the most directly affected by what happened. Would you please start us off?'

Theo spoke about his bruises, his medical treatment, and his fear of coming back to school. His parents supported these things, mentioned their own worries about his safety and added that he had lost time out of his studies and had fallen behind in some classes. They were even contemplating pulling him out of the school and placing him in a private school.

Each effect of the problem was noted on the white board at the end of spokes drawn emanating from the circle in which the problem had been named. The facilitator continued around the circle until everyone had spoken about the effect of the problem on himself or herself. For example, Aaron volunteered that he might be expelled from school and added that he did not want that to happen.

After a thorough exploration of the problem and its effects, the facilitator drew a second circle on the whiteboard and a new set of spokes emanating from it as well.

He then indicated the first circle and announced, 'This is the problem that brought us all here. It is a serious problem that has had some very serious effects. But no problem story ever tells us all that is to be known about a person or a situation. Now I am going to ask you to think about Aaron. What do you know about him that we would be blind to, if we only paid attention to this problem story? Can anyone tell me a story about him that does not fit with this problem?'

After a slight pause, Mike, the English teacher, described a situation in which he had watched Aaron in class taking the lead in a group journalism project and helping out other students when he had completed his own work. This was noted on the whiteboard at the end of one of the spokes emanating from the second circle.

The facilitator asked, 'What does that tell you about Aaron that is different from the problem story?'

Mike thought for a moment and said, 'He can certainly be responsible and helpful, rather than hurtful, when he wants to be.'

The facilitator wrote down 'responsible' and 'helpful' in the center of the circle.

Florence was the next to speak. She spoke of her loving grandson who had been her source of hope for the future of her family for years, because he was so bright and outgoing. Again the facilitator wrote down some of her words and asked what this story told her about Aaron that did not fit with the problem story.

Florence said he was kind, rather than violent, by nature. This was noted in the center of the circle.

The conversation continued around the circle with a series of stories about Aaron that made him seem less like a monster and more like someone who had made a mistake and done something wrong. Even Angelica, Theo's Mom, spoke about how Aaron and Theo used to be in the same youth group and had gotten along fine in the past. The list of stories around the outside of the circle grew, as did the list of positive qualities inside the circle. The tense and somber mood of the conference started to ease a little.

When the circle that represented the counter story had reached a sufficiently detailed point and everyone who wanted to had contributed to it, the facilitator moved to the next stage of the process. He addressed Aaron directly and asked him to look at the two circles and consider them carefully.

'Which of these two stories would you want everyone here to know about you in future?' he asked.

Aaron smiled slightly and pointed immediately to the second circle that had recorded elements of the counter story.

'Thank you,' said the facilitator and continued, 'Now our task is to work out a plan so that this problem story can fade away and this other story can grow big enough so that everyone here knows this to be more true of Aaron in the future.'

Everyone in the meeting was asked to contribute ideas that would help grow the counter story. To privilege the voice of the victim, the facilitator wanted to start with Theo again and with his parents. It can be very important that the victim's voice is heard first.

'You spoke earlier about how the problem left you, Theo, feeling afraid and you two, Albert and Angelica, feeling worried about your son's safety. What would need to happen to make the fear and worry go away?'

Albert was somewhat skeptical about how this could realistically happen because the pattern of aggression and bullying among Aaron and his friends was well-established.

'The first thing you need to do is to apologize for what you did,' Albert said directly to Aaron.

Aaron looked a little shamefaced and mumbled an apology.

'Thank you Aaron,' said the facilitator softly. 'Albert, how would you know whether this apology can be trusted?'

It was Angelica who answered.

'He needs to speak to his friends who were laughing while he attacked our son. It's not enough just to apologize to Theo. They need to hear too that he is ashamed for what he did. Assuming that he is actually sorry about it.'

'What about it, Aaron?' asked the facilitator.

Aaron was looking very awkward and did not quite know

what to say. In the end, with some help from Tina and Mike, he agreed to a ritual meeting with Theo and three of his friends, with his mother and his English teacher present, in which he would apologize again to Theo in front of his friends and formally ask his friends to be friendly toward Theo and ensure that he was safe from violence and bullying. Albert was not sure that Aaron would be able to do this. It was therefore decided in the meeting that Aaron would need to prepare a written statement of what he was going to say before the meeting and then read it aloud when the time came. Furthermore, the written statement would have to be vetted in advance by Albert and by the school principal before the meeting would be called.

The meeting continued to work on a number of further elements in the plan. Florence told Angelica that she was embarrassed about what her grandson had done. She reached out in sympathy for what Theo's family must have been going through and offered for two weeks to wait for her grandson and for Theo at the school gate each day after school and to ensure that no violence was taking place.

Laura, Aaron's social worker, offered to meet with Aaron every Friday for the next two months to talk about how he was going to step away from violence. Aaron was willing to do this. Tina expressed relief because she had been very worried about how Aaron was being influenced by the youth culture around him into being too interested in fighting and violence. She asked the school and the social worker for help to turn this trend around.

A system of monitoring the relationships between the boys

during school was discussed and Tina agreed to make phone contact with the counselor each week for the next term to check how Aaron was doing in class.

After all the adults had spoken, Theo made a brave little speech in which he told Aaron that what he had done was wrong and spoke about how he was not looking to become friends with Aaron, but he wanted to get along with him without needing to be afraid of any physical threats.

Aaron was squirming with awkwardness as he listened to Theo, but he heard him out and repeated his apology, this time wiping a tear from his eye. The meeting ended with handshakes between Aaron's family and Theo's.

The conference had a strong effect on Aaron. Doing the tasks he had been assigned were harder for him than handling any punishment the school might have handed out, but he did them. It was now significantly harder for him to embrace violence at school and he told his friends that he had to be more careful and respectful. They were a bit nonplussed but went along with the change.

This is a very different kind of story from the mediation described earlier, but the same principles are at work. The conversation needs to be more structured in a conference with twelve people present than in a mediation between two people but it is structured around the principle of contrasting a problem story and a counter story. In both cases, the counter story is also established first, before addressing the issues that need to be negotiated.

Moreover, in a conference context, both the problem story and the counter story are recognized as woven into the networks of a community. By contrast, many judicial and school disciplinary processes are focused solely on the individual, on whom all of the responsibility for change is concentrated. Externalizing language aids this shared involvement in the process of story construction. While Aaron was asked to make responsible personal choices toward the growth of a counter story, the invitation for him to do so comes wrapped in a cloak of community support, rather than individual blame. This deliberate emphasis is an expression of the social constructionist belief that personal narratives are not owned solely by individuals but are constructed in the process of social exchange.

A CONFLICT COACHING EXAMPLE

A third example of growing a counter story occurs in a counseling context where Manu, who is seventeen, tells his school counselor how he handled a conflict in his home during the weekend. Manu had intervened when his father had begun to physically abuse Manu's mother. Manu had stepped in between his father and his mother, but his father had not let his violent intention subside. Manu had fought with his father physically for about a minute, while calling to his mother to get away.

The whole incident was over in a few minutes. Manu's mother left quickly for her sister's place. Manu himself had run off and had walked the streets feeling very distressed for about four hours. When he had eventually come home, his father had gone to bed. Manu had been still seething, however, and had gone into his room and in a fit of anger, punched the wall. Manu showed his counselor the bruised and swollen hand and suspected that one of his fingers was broken.

As they reflected on what had happened, Manu remained proud of his effort to protect his mother, even though he did not like fighting with his father. He was disappointed with himself, however about punching the wall. The counselor was curious about this response.

'I don't want to feel so mad,' said Manu. 'It's like I am being just like my dad. Lashing out with my fist.'

The counselor recognized an opening here that could serve as a starting point for a counter story and inquired more into Manu's reasons for his disappointment with himself. She helped him articulate a preference for a different way of responding and a relationship value system that was not based on physical abuse.

'Is it like you are so familiar with your dad's example that you are afraid you will turn out just like him?' she guessed.

'Yes,' Manu admitted, his face full of emotion.

'That makes sense,' she mused, 'because your father's example is probably the one you know best. But you also have a choice about whether you want to follow that example or reject it.'

She was careful to use externalizing language here and speak about the 'bad example' rather than about Manu's father as a bad person. She also realized that it would be harder for him to concentrate on not following his father's example than it would to identify a more positive example to use as a model.

'I'm wondering whether you have any other examples to draw from?'

'What do you mean?' asked Manu.

'Is there any adult you are close to who has shown you a different way of behaving toward women that you could use as an example to follow?'

Manu responded immediately, 'My uncle.'

'Tell me about your uncle.'

'He's really cool. He has a boat and he takes me fishing.'

'So what have you noticed about how your uncle treats women?'

What followed was a long conversation about Manu and his uncle. Manu had actually carefully watched his uncle's relationship with his mother's sister. With his counselor's encouragement he made a thorough study of his uncle's actions. As many details as possible were accumulated of his uncle's calm demeanor and loving respect for his partner, even when they disagreed over things. Manu became quite animated while telling these stories. He spent a lot of time with his uncle and aunt and looked up to him a lot. His uncle was someone he could use as a model for the kind of person he was shaping himself into. He and his counselor developed a story of a different set of relational principles that he would prefer to fold into his own life and they proceeded to work at doing this.

Clearly what evolved was a counter story to the story of following his father's violent example. The counter story had been accessed this time by inquiring into other relationships that might serve as a model for development. He was not even required to stop loving his father. Nor did he abandon his pride in having stood up to protect his mother. He just made a decision to model his own behavior on someone else whose values he admired. This is another way to acknowledge the narrative assumption that multiple storylines always exist.

PRINCIPLES FOR GROWING A COUNTER STORY

In each of the examples cited above, the professional starts from the assumption that a different story of relationship will always exist if we care to inquire into it. This core belief is founded on the sheer complexity of life. Even when they are hard at first to identify, small exceptions to a conflict story will always be found somewhere.

Conflict resolution practitioners need to remain alert to the spontaneous appearance of moments of difference or unique outcomes. These moments can be identified through careful double listening. If they are not appearing spontaneously, the next option is to ask about their existence. If they still do not show themselves, one might ask again, or phrase the question differently, or inquire in some other place.

Another important principle of narrative practice is the exercise of curiosity. Curiosity turns a moment inside-out to reveal its richness, its connections with other moments and it creative force. As Michel Foucault (1989) says of curiosity,

> ... it evokes 'concern'; it evokes the care one takes for what exists and could exist; an acute sense of the real which, however, never becomes fixed; a readiness to find our surroundings strange and singular; a certain relentlessness

in ridding ourselves of our familiarities and looking at things otherwise; a passion for seizing what is happening now and what is passing away; a lack of respect for traditional hierarchies of the important and the essential. (p. 305.)

Such curiosity renders significant momentary flickerings of life that might otherwise disappear and makes them last longer, signify more, and have greater influence.

The next principle is an aesthetic appreciation of a well-formed story. Once a unique outcome has been identified, it must be grown into a viable and well-formed story. A well-formed story contains a series of plot events that occupy the dimension of time. It is organized around some degree of thematic consistency, rather than remaining a haphazard sequence of chance events. It contains details of setting and context and is associated with some form of characterization of persons and relationships. The curiosity mentioned above is most useful if it is turned to the purpose of constructing such a story. This means a deliberate effort to inquire into the following:

- *the history that a unique outcome represents*
- *the sequence of decisions, actions and reactions that make up a single plot event*
- *the values, commitments, hopes, dreams, and treasured principles that a unique outcome embodies*
- *the meanings, significations, importance and rationale that can be attributed to an action of difference*
- *the most apt name for the counter story*

If all of these principles are enjoined, then chances are that a viable relationship counter story to a conflict story will emerge. Once it has some degree of viability, it can serve as the basis for resolving any outstanding issues that might need to be negotiated. That will be the focus of the next chapter.

SUMMARY FOCUS

- Life is more complex than can be contained in any one story.

- Unique outcomes always exist.

- Anything people are unhappy about implies its opposite—what they would prefer.

- We can inquire into what people would prefer, or into a moment that indicates what they would prefer.

- Such inquiry requires persistence and curiosity.

- A counter story to a conflict story might be organized around a relationship theme like cooperation, respect, understanding, peace, etc.

- A counter story always has a history that can be traced and rests upon a foundation of cherished values and commitments that can be articulated.

- To be viable a counter story should be articulated as a well-formed story.

- A viable counter story can serve as the foundation upon which outstanding issues can be negotiated.

CHAPTER 6

SUSTAINING CHANGE

T HE CONFLICTUAL FORCES THAT KEEP everyone entrenched in the problem story are numerous. They are also powerful and unlikely to surrender to the first counter story that comes along. People who are stuck in an unpleasant, destructive conflict often struggle to escape its clutches, because they have become convinced of their own perspective within the conflict as true, or at the very least as advantageous or preferred. For them, resolving the conflict can feel like denying their own truth claims, or surrendering a position of righteous indignation, and they fear ending up in a less advantageous position if they were to participate in making an agreement. Conflicts are further intensified by the ease with which people pathologize the other party. They also tend to portray their own participation in the conflict in benign terms while simultaneously assigning malevolent intentions to the other.

In some forms of mediation and conflict resolution practice, agreements and settlements are achieved with grudging effort only to be quickly unraveled in the face of ongoing disrespect and distrust after the mediation ends. It is a challenge to sustain a story of cooperation and understanding in the face of strong pulls to revert to pathologizing and blame.

Mediators are not immune from the forces that engage people in conflict stories and can be enlisted to view problem situations in rigid and narrow terms. People in conflict are often creative in their invitations to the mediator to pathologize and demonize the other. When the mediator gets caught up in blaming perspectives he or she can lose the ability to take an even-handed and curious posture and is thus denied the creativity and flexibility essential to responding to challenging conflict.

The underlying premise of this chapter is that sustaining desirable change is most likely to occur when a narrative of relational change starts to become embedded rather than focused on a single moment of agreement. A counter-narrative to a conflict narrative needs to be sustained through time and lived out, rather than focused on one settlement event. Its plot needs to be thickened, its characters developed and its themes elaborated.

For this to happen, parties need to replace pathologizing, negative, narrow and rigid assessments of each other with richer, more comprehensive and more empathetic recognition of the motives and purposes of those with whom they were in conflict. This chapter's major thrust is to articulate the mediator's critical role in building more nuanced and empathetic knowing between conflicted parties and elaborating a counter narrative of relationship grounded in this enriched understanding. Achieving this understanding involves, in part, continuing to be curious about what has been at stake for the parties and about the motivating forces that shape divergent viewpoints and differing opinions. And it involves enriching the narrative of relationship to include more and more details of what has hitherto been excluded from consideration. Henry Wadsworth Longfellow states it this way:

> *If we could read the secret history of our enemies, we should find in each man's life sorrow and suffering enough to disarm all hostility.* (2000, p. 797).

Longfellow is making the point that mutual understanding and respect can be gained by getting to know the other person outside the conflict story. Doing so can soften the defensive position people tend to take in conflict situations. It also reiterates the narrative assumption that multiple storylines always exist. Appreciating these storylines can motivate people to create an alternative, more preferable story of their relationship, no longer dominated by conflict.

A FANTASY STORY

In contrast to earlier chapters some of the principles of narrative mediation will be described in a rather novel way by using a fairytale as illustration.

> *One sunny morning, in a far away world, a big frog decided to swallow all of the water of the earth. It sat there looking proud and full. It looked like a mountain of water, blue, and green, its skin almost transparent under the tension.*

It could not move; it was too heavy. So it just sat there, staring at all the animals and humans gathered in front of it.

'What are we going to do?' cried all the living beings. 'We will all die if it does not give back the rivers, brooks, and oceans.'

For three days, they prayed and begged the frog to let go of the waters but the frog would not move. The children were crying, the elderly suffering, and the desert sand could be seen creeping closer to the horizon. Something had to be done.

Translated and adapted from Gougaud (2000 as cited in Beaudoin, & Taylor. 2009, p. 8)

Imagine you are a mediator who wants to help the frog and the animals and humans resolve the conflict. It would probably be difficult to embody a dispassionate, unaffected stance as you addressed this suffering. You are motivated to ensure that no harm befalls the animals and humans suffering from this egregious act. You might even feel tempted to force the frog to release the water, as this action would immediately satisfy one very large collective. The immediate crisis would be averted, but there would remain the possibility of it re-occurring, if the issues which produced the conflict in the first place are not addressed. Let's playfully apply some narrative strategies to address the conflict and to create sustainable change.

In any conflict, it takes very little for parties affected by conflict to further elaborate upon the problem-saturated narrative. Both parties typically pathologize one another, portraying their own participation in the conflict in benign terms and assigning malevolent intentions to the party they are in conflict with. It is easy to attack the frog, because it seems obvious who the malevolent actor is. To guard against getting lost within the pathologizing narrative, it is important for a mediator to start from the assumption that all parties' actions must make sense in their own terms.

The first task is therefore to inquire into and show respect for the background events that have produced the conflict. A persistently curious stance is needed to explore the parties' unexpressed statements and hinted-at comments; to unearth the background cultural forces at work; and to inquire into the unarticulated hopes, intentions and values. The mediator might ask questions such as:

- *What do you want to achieve?*
- *What circumstances motivated you to take these actions?*
- *What needs or desires were demanding that you satisfy them?*
- *What kind of identity do you want to perform in the world?*
- *Right now, how are you being affected by the actions you have taken?*

The mediator learns that the frog, like the animals and humans, has been clinging to life but now is unable to breathe properly, move around, eat or do what frogs like to do. The frog might even drown under the weight of the water. The mediator asks the frog whether or not it wants to live. The frog signals that it wishes to release the water safely and avoid producing further chaos for itself, or for the animals and humans. The immediate settlement interrupts the drama of the crisis, but does not in itself constitute a new narrative.

To generate a new narrative of relationship between the frog and the animals and humans the mediator has more work to do. This work will involve tracing the history of what led to the crisis in the first place and double listening while doing so. Tracking the trajectory of the parties' concerns and values from the past through the present and into the future can open up some new lines to follow that do not lead towards the same kind of dramatic stand-off. Establishing these new trajectories of relationship can generate an ongoing narrative of resolution, rather than just an aversion of the immediate crisis. The mediator invites the animals and humans to share their perspectives, ideas, hopes and values by asking them questions such as:

- *What circumstances are motivating you to want to live life uninterrupted by the action of the frog?*
- *What kind of life were you living and what would you hope to sustain?*
- *What is your understanding of what has created the problem for the frog in the first place?*
- *What actions have you taken to try to resolve this struggle?*
- *What can you contribute to help resolve this situation?*
- *What drove you to beg the frog to let go of the waters?*

At this point, richer descriptions needed to be accessed to create the context for sustainable change. The stage had to be set for a relationship narrative that would be incompatible with the conflict continuing. Building this narrative would require respectful and careful double listening, as well as the use of empathy to produce more nuanced understandings of relations between the frog and the human and animal communities.

According to the frog, the animals and humans had been contaminating the water for many years. The water was now polluted to almost intolerable proportions to the point that all life had been threatened with extinction. The frog demonstrated greater sensitivity than the animals and humans to the increased pollution of what was, after all, the frog's habitat. It could not take it any longer. Many other frogs had fallen sick and died well before their time. Baby frogs were dying because of the toxins produced by the animals' and humans' lifestyles. To date, all the frog's prior pleas to stop poisoning the environment had been ignored by the collective community. As an act of last resort, therefore, the frog had felt compelled to take some radical steps to avert impending doom.

The humans agreed they had been caught up unconsciously in an addictive cycle of consumption to feed their immediate desires, which they knew were rapidly depleting resources. They agreed that they had been deaf to the frog's pleas. The actions of the frog had precipitated a crisis that could be seen as a wake-up call. It even encouraged the other animals and humans to debate among themselves their own participation in the pollution crisis. They said that they had been caught up in vicious forces that had prompted them to accumulate objects to make themselves appear more important and somehow more worthy than all other animals. They knew that this accumulation of objects would be difficult to give up, but they were developing more empathy with the frog community as they contemplated how they might inevitably suffer the same fate already befalling the frogs.

Differing viewpoints arose among the animals who defined themselves as 'wild' and those who were clearly domesticated by humans. The domesticated animals were accused of colluding with the humans. Also paws and claws were pointed at some other animals who had been quietly benefiting from the environment of consumption through their scavenging. Meanwhile representatives from some endangered species made passionate appeals to take the frog seriously. It was becoming more and more clear that there were multiple perspectives on the crisis. In the end, the animals and humans decided that choosing a long and healthy life was preferable to the ongoing accumulation and acquisition of shiny objects and started to acknowledge the concerns of the frog community.

The mediator now began to ask questions to grow this fledgling narrative of acknowledgment into one that could fly (the bird community were especially keen to support this idea). Questions were asked about the history of ideas of interdependence. Values that had a history in human and animal communities were inquired into. Some forgotten values of conservation and of respect for other species began to be mentioned.

The mediator asked, 'What specific actions might you all undertake to embody the idea of sustainability on the ground?'

After hearing a range of responses, the mediator turned to the frog and asked whether what he was hearing made any difference.

'Yes it does,' croaked the frog.

'What difference does it make?'

'Well it means we can work together more and I won't have to resort to extreme measures to get my plight noticed.'

Gradually a commitment to mutual survival began to take form. Moreover, all parties showed interest in working with the mediator to explore courses of action that would both protect the environment on the one hand, and provide the necessary resources to sustain them on the other. Now that understandings had been reached about what was motivating all of the parties' actions, the mediator was in a good position to begin a brainstorming process of working out plans, strategies and activities that would meet the shared understandings of a way forward to resolve outstanding problems.

It is only from a position within a narrative of mutual respect and understanding that there could be any real chance of sustaining a story of cooperation and agreement. Forced agreements can easily lead to a reversion to old behaviors and actions and the ascription to pathologizing and blameworthy intentions of others. In the end, the mediator proposed the drawing up of a charter that all the humans and animals could abide by that would document the mutual understanding that the meeting had generated.

We hope this fantasy story serves the purpose in showcasing the important narrative principles that might sustain alternative narratives in the face of challenging conflict. Here some of the narrative principles referred to in this story:

- *When someone takes extreme action assume that in some way it makes sense in the mind of the individual concerned. Inquire further into what an expression of anger might be protesting about.*
- *Be curious about the purposes, hopes, and actions either directly expressed or intimated by parties trapped in conflict.*
- *Double listen for thoughts, expressions and actions that provide the basis for the production of narratives leading towards mutual understanding, empathy, respect and resolution.*
- *Pay attention to the background cultural narratives that inform the parties' positions in the conflict instead of being swept up by narrow, thin descriptions the conflict.*
- *Externalize the conflict and explore its effects on persons (and animals).*
- *Develop richer, more nuanced, and more complex understandings of what has happened.*
- *Focus on differences that emerge between versions of the story of relationship between the parties that have been nurtured by the conflict itself and emergent versions that feature greater understanding, cooperation and respect.*
- *Inquire into the history of counter-narratives to strengthen parties' commitments to these.*
- *Be curious about the values, commitments, principles, and cherished purposes that underlie actions that promise a different relationship story.*
- *Be curious too about values, commitments, principles, and cherished purposes that parties espouse out loud and ask for specific details of concrete actions on the ground that illustrate these themes.*
- *Document for future reference the developments that a mediation conversation produces.*

For the rest of this chapter we shall address some specific practices that help grow and extend narratives that run in different directions and produce different futures from dominating conflict narratives.

SUSTAINING COUNTER NARRATIVES IN DIVORCE MEDIATION

One very common feature of divorce between intimate partners with children is that the conflict between the adults becomes mixed up in battles over the parenting of the children. Usually the divorce results from breakdown in the relationship between the spouses and from there contaminates relationships with the children as well.

In our first book on narrative mediation (Winslade, & Monk, 2000), we published some firsthand comments from children who were old enough to articulate how much they preferred their parents not to involve them in adult conflicts. When parents do manage to protect children from the pain and bitterness that they as parents are going through, the children do not experience as much distress from the family disruption that divorce produces (Emery, 1995).

In one sense, it is understandable that the contamination of parenting by spousal conflicts might happen, because being a spouse and being a parent are closely intertwined and are both deeply implicated in personal identity. There are nevertheless important distinctions that can be drawn between a couple's relationship as partners and their relationship as parents. Before a separation this distinction is not so important to make but after separation it can become critical (especially to the children's wellbeing) to do so. One of the key transitions that divorce represents is the separation of parenting from partnering. The spousal partnership is ending but, in most cases, the parenting does not, or should not, end. Both parties to the divorce are still parents of the children, even though they no longer live together as partners.

Many people stumble over this transition, however. The frustration and anguish they feel from their conflict as partners spills over into arguments about the children. Some fathers walk away from their responsibilities as parents and others suddenly become interested in the parenting that they have previously left to their wives. Some women draw their children around them and work against the children's relationships with their fathers and others criticize every move their former spouses make as parents or resent their former husbands' new found interest in being fathers.

In these situations, it can be useful in mediation to help a couple make clear distinctions between the narrative of their relationship as partners and the narrative of their relationship as parents. A foundational narrative principle on which this distinction is based is that we are all multi-storied. A simple extension of this idea is that our relationships are multi-storied as well. We do not just have one relationship narrative, as many people think. We might have one relationship narrative as spouses, and another as parents. Sometimes the narrative that governs how a couple might work together as parents might be strong and unproblematic even though the narrative that governs their life as intimate partners is flawed to the extent that they cannot contemplate living together any more.

Once this distinction has been made, the counter story of conciliation can be focused on and limited to the narrative of ongoing relationship as parents. The spousal conflict story can be externalized and inquiry can attend to the undermining effect this story (rather than either of the persons involved) is attempting to have on the parenting narrative. To be sure, this parenting narrative is in transition, but is often not under threat of extinction in the same way as the spousal relationship narrative.

Here are some suggested lines of inquiry that might be built on this distinction:

- *I understand that you are divorcing each other as spouses but I don't believe either of you intends to divorce the children. Is that right? Can you explain why?*

- *What kind of relationship as co-parents do your children deserve you to work at? Is it in your mutual interest to work toward that kind of relationship as parents or not?*

- *How do you both hope you can protect your children from the effects of the differences between you as spouses?*

- *Have you noticed any ways in which the conflict between you as spouses has tried to interfere with your working with each other as parents?*

- *How are you working to save the parenting of your children from the threat of being overwhelmed by the conflict between you as spouses?*

- *Which topics of conversation now belong off limits in your relationship as parents, rather than as spouses?*

Which topics of conversation are important for you to have for your children's sake, despite the conflict between you as spouses?

- *Can you think of any examples when you have worked together as parents since the separation as well as you did before it?*

- *How would you both rate your overall level of cooperation as parents, if 1 was serious problems with cooperation and 10 was excellent cooperation?*

- *How have you been able to achieve a 5 (for example) when you have been subjected to such difficult challenges that normally accomplish a separation?*

THE ROLE OF APOLOGIES IN SUSTAINING CHANGE

Apologies are clearly important to the growth of counter stories. They can resurrect reputations that have been hurt and often initiate the embracing of preferred identities. In conflict, many of us wait for an apology from people who have hurt, humiliated or shamed us. The hope is that an apology from the other will allow us to put to rest bad feelings we have towards that person and move on.

If such an apology is not forthcoming, it is tempting to pathologize those who have hurt us. Cooperative narratives of relationship are easily disrupted by a single action or by a few misunderstood words and quickly replaced with powerful blaming narratives. Based upon these narratives, strong ultimatums, totalizing attributions, and decisions to foreclose on relationship are then elaborated. Here are some examples:

- *He was so rude and abusive! I will never have anything to do with him again!*

- *I pretend everything is just fine with my colleague, but I avoid her at all costs. I will never forgive her for what she did!*

- *I felt so humiliated when I heard how they talked about me behind my back. I can't even say anything to them. I feel sick to my stomach.*

- *We work on the same team but I will never really share my creative ideas freely again. It really is their loss.*

- *She doesn't get it. I hate her. I am consumed by hate when she walks in the room.*

In the face of such statements, the task of a mediation conversation is to acknowledge the hurt that has been produced but also to render these statements contingent upon events. They represent one possible story of relationship linked to a particular set of events. There are multiple other storylines that exist, however, and these can be resurrected or initiated.

Once a counter story has been breached, it often happens that one or other of the parties makes an apology for what they have said or done in the conflict story. On other occasions, someone might not be willing to go as far as making an apology for fear of appearing to shoulder too much of the blame, but he or she is willing to offer at least a heartfelt acknowledgement of the pain that the conflict has caused to the other. Such gestures are unique outcomes in the context of the conflict story.

Apologies or gestures of heartfelt acknowledgement present the other person, however, with a dilemma. Is the apology trustworthy or is it just a form of words? Is it a cynical attempt to get out of the line of fire in the conflict, or is it a genuine effort to set the relationship onto a different footing? Does it make a significant difference or is it just a set of empty words when different forms of action are needed? Should an apology just be accepted for what it is or does it imply that the other person should immediately forgive? If I accept this apology, am I being naïve or generous?

The dominant Judeo-Christian discourse stresses the importance of apology and creates a pressure for the recipient of the apology to forgive in return. Apology promises freedom from the negative thoughts that might otherwise pervade the lives of those who hang on to anger until it turns to bitterness. Forgiveness similarly promises freedom from ongoing resentment and opens the possibility of being in charge of our lives again. Unwillingness to let go and to put the past behind us, on the other hand, promises a diminished life constrained by growing hatred, fear, and anxiety.

If we think in narrative terms, the dilemmas around apology and forgiveness are eased. It is common for people to assume that an apology should end the conflict story. But an apology (or for that matter, a gesture of forgiveness) is better thought of as a move into a possible counter story than as a conclusion of a conflict story. Narrative practice suggests that it is, however, only one plot event in that story. On its own, it does not amount to a story of difference that can be trusted to survive very long. In order for it to become a viable story, in order for it to prove itself trustworthy, it needs to be linked with other plot events in that story. The narrative needs to be fleshed out. In particular, the words of the apology need to be linked with actions that follow from it. Narrative mediators might therefore ask some questions about an apology. For example:

- *In the spirit of that apology, what do you plan to do differently?*

- *What might you need to see happening before you could be satisfied that his apology was genuine?*

- *How might you both build on that apology so that it could never be looked back on as empty words?*

In each of these questions the assumption is that the story needs to be elaborated by locating the apology in a trajectory of difference in which it is linked to other plot events, other gestures of restored relationship. Let us illustrate these principles with a story.

A newly appointed principal, Alexa Sharples, invited Doug Laskey, a talented teacher, to introduce a restorative model of discipline in their middle school. The school had high suspension and expulsion rates. Alexa Sharples had developed a strong reputation in a nearby school for innovative school and community initiatives and Doug Laskey was experienced with applying narrative restorative justice work in schools.

A small team working with Doug engaged in a series of productive meetings with Alexa. A high level of respect and synergy was built up in these meetings and the team members expressed appreciation of Alexa's willingness to engage in innovative discipline practices. A local private charity even came forward to fund the restorative justice project in the school. The funding was substantial and the donor stipulated that the money had to be spent on the project within the next few months.

Soon after, Alexa became distracted by difficult school district politics and the restorative practice initiative was temporarily placed on hold. She was fielding criticism about changes she was making in the school and some staff members were pushing back about new expectations introduced by her.

Meanwhile, Doug had invested a lot of time planning and developing Restorative Practices Training materials and he and his team now had to sit and wait for the word from Alexa to proceed. Doug was frustrated because the funding deadline was rapidly approaching. To explain the delay, Doug mentioned to his team that Alexa had got caught up in some difficult local politics and had become distracted. He concluded that the restorative practices project might not proceed.

The relationship between Doug and Alexa deteriorated. Alexa was not responding to Doug's calls to set up meetings. Doug was hearing from colleagues that Alexa was waiting for Doug to get the team organized. They were not talking but were now at cross-purposes.

Alexa was offended to hear that Doug had criticized her in the community. She felt she was being blamed for stopping the project. Doug was shocked to hear this information and was certain that he had not done anything wrong. Nor did he believe he had spoken critically of Alexa. The two of them were at a stand-off;

the project was now immobilized; goodwill seemed to have evaporated; and the project was at risk of losing its funding.

Through a narrative lens we can see that the story of a cooperative, trusting, respectful relationship was being eclipsed by another relationship narrative that was saturated in conflict. The project was now stuck and the conflict was having effects on everyone. Team members were losing trust, cooperation was diminishing, and disrespect was growing. Alexa felt that her good reputation was being damaged by negative gossip. Doug felt misunderstood and that his words had been mischaracterized, leading to the finger of blame being pointed at him.

At stake in the conflict were cherished identity commitments and a concern about the reputation that both Alexa and Doug might accrue in the eyes of others. Identity commitments and reputations are often tightly interwoven in the narratives that give shape to conflicts. When these are under attack, sustaining a counter story will be difficult and engaging cooperatively in creative actions will be unlikely. What was needed were new opportunities for Alexa and Doug to reclaim their reputations and be acknowledged for their identities. Something needed to shift.

Doug sought out conflict coaching from a trusted colleague and recognized that getting the project moving again would require addressing the issues of hurt. Doug wanted the goodwill, team spirit and synergy to return and started to think about what he could do that would make this possible. He decided to take his own hurt feelings in hand and approach Alexa in an effort to mend the relationship. He was prepared to acknowledge the role he had played in Alexa's distress. 'Alexa,' he began when they met with the assistance of a mediator, 'I have clearly done some things that hurt you. It was not my intention but I have to acknowledge that I spoke out of turn to others and was careless with the words I used. I allowed my frustration with the situation to influence how I came across and to sound like I was blaming it on you. I understand now, although I didn't at the time, how this was hurtful for you and interfered with what you were trying to manage. I regret all this, but I can't take it back now. I would like, however, to ask you whether it is possible for us to return to where we were, or somewhere close to it, and continue working together on the project.'

Alexa had attended the meeting with some misgivings, and was a little surprised by Doug's comments. But she was moved by them. She saw in front of her the choice between continuing to speak from the defensive position of nurturing her sense of hurt or of responding to Doug's overture. Alexa weighed her thoughts for a minute. She had been reminded of the cooperative relationship story that she and Doug had been building and to herself she acknowledged that. She was also conscious of her own position as a school leader and asked herself what a good leader might do in this situation.

'Thank you, Doug,' Alexa said eventually. 'I appreciate what it took to say that. I was distressed by what happened and was embarrassed by what you said. But I appreciate your saying that you regret it now. You are right that we can't turn back the clock. The damage has been done. But it is not damage that cannot be repaired. I acknowledge that I too have not handled this situation as I would have preferred. I was probably too quick to heap blame on you without discussing with you what had happened. I also acknowledge that I caused you a frustrating delay without giving you much explanation. I am sorry about that and sorry that all that happened has damaged our work on the restorative practices project. I too would like to put that behind us, if we can, and get back to working together.'

This exchange clearly opened the door for a shift to a different relationship narrative. To capitalize on it, had a mediator worked with Alexa and Doug, she or he could have asked some further questions to strengthen the narrative of cooperation. Questions with impact might involve reaching back into the past and also building the narrative forward into the future. Here are some examples:

- *Doug, what was it about your relationship with Alexa in the past that prompted you to believe it might be worthwhile taking this initiative today?*

- *Alexa, when you paused before speaking, you seemed to be weighing up options for responding. Was that right and, if so, what convinced you to make the choice you did?*

- *What needs to happen now to take this new understanding you have reached and embody it in action?*

- *Is there any damage that has been done by the conflict that still needs addressing?*

- *Who else needs to be involved in this new story you are creating and how might they be invited to join it?*

NARRATIVE LETTER WRITING

A final goal in this chapter is to illustrate the narrative practice of documenting developments in mediation and giving such documents back to the parties concerned (White, & Epston, 1990; Winslade, & Monk, 2000). It is common practice in mediation to do this with written settlements or agreements, but narrative practice is aimed at more than a settlement. It is concerned with an ongoing narrative of agreement formulated into a counter story. This story is likely to contain much more that can be documented than what is included in a final agreement. Here is an example of a letter written between two meetings in a family mediation that attends to progress made in the first meeting and looks forward to a subsequent meeting. It is a letter written by Simon Everington, a student of narrative mediation.

Dear Hannah and Tim,

Before we next meet, I wanted to write to you and offer an overview of what we have covered so far, what you have achieved, and what remains outstanding.

A series of challenging events have caused both of you considerable concern, to the extent that you have decided to live apart. It has inflicted anxiety in your relationship, particularly fear of poverty and anxiety about Laura's (their daughter) *wellbeing.*

And yet, you both expressed admiration and respect for each other. Until recently, you had been very happy together. Hannah, you said that you 'just wanted to forget everything and to live in a happy family again'. Tim, you had some doubt about whether this was possible just yet, but you did express the strong desire 'to interact without any problem.'

Hannah, you told us how the dispute has led to feelings of guilt, both in terms of your commitments to Tim and Laura, and to your mother, brothers and sister. These concerns have isolated you from them, and have caused worry about Laura's wellbeing. This was making it difficult for you to talk to Tim.

Tim, you explained how the dispute has caused you disappointment. You do not just want a return to things as they were, but a greater mutual respect between all members of both families. You want everyone to accept each other and to work to create a loving family environment in which Laura can grow up happily and safely. The dispute was preventing this from happening.

You both, nevertheless, expressed willingness to explore these problems in the 'hope that something can change'. You also suggested ideas about how to move forwards, which were:

- *That both families sit together to discuss each others' feelings and perspectives on how to overcome the fear of poverty.*

- *Hannah, you have asked Tim to return to live in your home again.*

- *Tim, you appreciated that this would help save you money if you no longer have to pay rent at the place where you currently live.*

- *You jointly agreed to spend more time together with Laura to look after her needs and to work on your relationship.*

I am still wondering how much these steps might affect your concerns. I also have a few ongoing questions for you to consider before next week:

- *Do these agreements mean that you are working towards re-establishing the relationships that you would prefer?*

- *How might improvements in family relationships and living together again impact on the fear of poverty that has affected you?*

- *Have there been any hints of these happening that we can discuss next week?*

I look forward to talking through your thoughts on these and other ideas next Friday.

Sincerely,

Simon.

Several points are worth noting about this letter. First, the second paragraph uses the narrative language of externalizing to refer to the conflict as 'a series of challenging events' and as 'it', in an effort to prolong the effect of this language for the parties.

Secondly, the problem situation is blamed (rather than either of the parties) for the effects of the problem. Again the letter aims to keep alive what has been breached in the meeting but may by now have been forgotten, were it not for this reminder.

Thirdly, the letter includes verbatim some of the key words used by the parties, thereby allowing them to reverberate longer.

Fourthly, the mediator makes reference to the elements of a counter story that have emerged in contrast to the conflict story. This story is represented through reference to a general spirit of willingness and expressions of hope. It is also linked to some suggestions, which are not yet agreements but are clearly under consideration. Each of these suggestions may become plot events in the counter story with clear links to the general spirit of willingness and hope.

Finally, the mediator offers some further questions in the letter for the parties to contemplate before the next meeting. These questions seek to add to the significance of the possible plot of the counter story and also to invite the parties to generate further developments in this plot.

SUMMARY FOCUS

- When mediators get caught up in the blaming perspectives of parties in conflict, an even-handed and curious posture can be lost. These actions can lead to a loss of creativity and flexibility necessary to address challenging conflict.

- A counter-narrative to a conflict narrative is dependent upon numerous non-conflictual events. The plot, characters, theme and storyline of the counter-narrative must be developed, thickened and elaborated upon.

- The development of a narrative of mutual respect and understanding is essential to sustaining a story of cooperation and agreement.

- Agreements that are forced or established within a hostile environment are often quickly reversed and pathologizing and blameworthy intentions re-emerge.

- Single narratives cannot contain who we are in the world and the relationships we engage in. Our identities and relationships are multi-faceted and multi-storied.

- To apologize and forgive is one step or plot event in a possible counter story rather than the conclusion of a conflict narrative.

- Efforts to re-establish trust following an apology need to be linked with other plot events that support a narrative of trust. Put simply, the words of the apology build trust to the extent that they are linked with actions that follow it.

CHAPTER 7
USING SKILLS PURPOSEFULLY

A T THE HEART OF ALL conflict resolution work is the investment of all parties (including third party mediators) in producing change. Good faith efforts to resolve conflict rest upon the desire to move past the entanglements, frustrations, and ragged circumstances that occur when conversations get stuck. Even though mediators play down any influential role in order to avoid accusations of coercion, they do have an interest in conflicted parties making changes toward greater mutual understanding and agreement.

It is, therefore, worth ending this book with a brief focus on the process of change. For many years we have been struck by the connections between the work developed by Miller and Rollnick (2002) on *motivational interviewing* and our work on narrative mediation. In this chapter, we seek to record some of the links between narrative mediation and some concepts drawn from motivational interviewing which can assist mediators to think through the phases that build momentum toward helpful change in conflict situations.

Miller and Rollnick argue that change rarely happens as a result of a simple yes or no decision but through a multifaceted, dynamic process dominated by tension, ambivalence, and uncertainty. It is difficult, for example, to make changes and do something different, because in doing so we might lose out on the benefits of not changing. Narrative practitioners understand this complexity and represent it as multiple narratives competing for attention.

For Miller and Rollnick, the motivation to make changes is not something produced in the heart of individuals but in their interaction with others. Motivation fluctuates according to how hospitable or not the conditions of the conversation are toward the idea of change. As social constructionists, we support this idea. The trick is for mediators, as for counseling practitioners, to match the skills of practice with the kind of conversation needed at a particular moment to increase the motivation for embracing a counter story. At some moments people are nowhere near accepting the need for change. Perhaps they still cannot imagine that a change might bring them more benefit than continuing to defend the conflict story. To push for a counter story at this moment would be coercive. At other moments, people have moved decisively toward a commitment to change and now need to focus their attention on strategies for change. To ask them to go back and examine the effects of the conflict story at this moment would irritate and confuse them. What is needed, therefore, is to link the conversational emphasis with where people are up to in the cycle of change.

Prochaska, DiClemente, and Norcross (1992) break down the process of change into a series of logical steps: *pre-contemplation, contemplation, preparation, action, maintenance and termination*. With regard to conflict, pre-contemplation is the stage when people are caught up in the conflict itself without any thought entering their heads about resolving differences. Contemplation is the stage where they start to become concerned about the conflict and are considering taking action to resolve it, but are not yet decided to do so. In the preparation phase, they have decided that resolution would be preferable and are debating with themselves or with others the best strategies for resolution. Once this decision about best strategy is made, the action phase of movement for change is engaged. But the first flush of enthusiasm for change can wear off and, therefore, in the next phase attention needs to shift to maintaining the ongoing change and knitting it into the fabric of living. Once a change has been stabilized, one can exit from the process of change.

There are a number of basic assumptions shared by motivational interviewing and narrative practice. As in motivational interviewing, narrative mediation practices need to be calibrated with where people are up to in the phases of change, in order to maximize motivation for, and efficient movement towards, change. Also, as in motivational interviewing, narrative mediation emphasizes respecting clients' decisions about where they are in the change process and acknowledging the complexity and difficulty of problem situations. Also like motivational interviewing, narrative practice does not find fault with ambivalence but recognizes it as a common experience when making sense of multiple stories. Both approaches also emphasize having faith in the resiliency of human beings rather than resorting to deficit-based pathologizing. Both also encourage practitioners to take a curious stance and to value collaboration, on the assumption that people are experts on their own lives and have a right to make autonomous choices.

We shall now link the stages of change with the particular narrative practices that most clearly facilitate motivation for and movement toward change.

PRE-CONTEMPLATION: In the pre-contemplation phase, people may not yet have recognized that there are things they are doing that could be modified. Typically they are so focused upon the other party as the source of the problem that they are not conscious of the possibility of multiple stories. Motivational interviewing has parties reviewing the evidence for what is contributing to the problem. In narrative mediation, one reason for preferring initial separate meetings with both parties is that often one party may be contemplating conflict resolution, while the other party is still in pre-contemplation. Separate meetings give the chance to raise the problem of the conflict and invite people to move into contemplation of some form of resolution.

Narrative practice uses double listening to spotlight competing stories. It is important at this stage not to foreclose on change by reassuring people or moving too quickly to strategies for resolution, before people have generated motivation to pursue it. Empathizing with the experience of ambivalence and asking questions that increase the sense of dilemma will help people move toward greater contemplation of change—the next stage in the process.

CONTEMPLATION: In the contemplation phase, the interactions between the practitioner and parties focus first on exploring the conflict story. People can be pulled by both poles of the binary of conflict - escalation and resolution. On one side of the dilemma, a person may be stuck in the dominant narrative, in which she is a benign actor caught in a problem of somebody else's making. She believes that the situation will only improve when the other person takes responsibility for causing the problem. On the other side of the dilemma, she is becoming better informed about the multiple narratives that are influencing the conflict and is entertaining the idea of engaging in new action. The motivation toward new action generally arises only after examining the toll the conflict is taking and the prospect of allowing the conflict to continue unchecked appears increasingly unviable.

Externalizing conversations advance the process of contemplation, because they place the conflict in the middle of the room, where it can be squarely looked at. Moreover, the discipline of externalizing pulls the practitioner, as well as the parties, away from the pathologizing impulse that locates problems within people's broken characters and personalities. The narrative technique of mapping the effects of problems on persons then increases the leverage for change, especially when the conversation reveals how these effects are diminishing choices, rather than expanding them. It will often bring people to the point of willingness to sacrifice the known and familiar for what is possible to know. Indignation at what a conflict might be doing is often sufficient to instigate a small rebellion against the belief that resolving a conflict amounts to giving in to another's demands. Change occurs when people believe the reasons for change outweigh the reasons against change.

In narrative mediation, the process of contemplation culminates in asking parties to evaluate the conflict and its effects. 'Is all this acceptable to you or not?' This direct inquiry invites the resolving of the dilemma in favor of either allowing the conflict story to continue unabated or of moving toward something different. When people state a preference for a new course of action, they step across the threshold of the doorway to change and enter the room where the preparation phase takes place. Now the mediator's focus changes. It is no longer about exploring the conflict story, but is focused on growing the counter story. People may be asked to argue for change by being asked the question, 'Why would you prefer to resolve things?' Answering this question involves taking a further step into the counter story.

Prochaska et. al. (1992) when discussing the stages of change describe the preparation phase as where people strategize for change before they take action to make it happen (the next phase). In narrative practice there is a movement back and forth between these two phases. The logic here is that action will be more likely to be productive if it already has a history in the particular ecology of people's lives and relationships. Hence, narrative practitioners often seek out unique outcomes that have already happened and attempt to grow these into a narrative that carries people forward into the action phase. Double listening has often already shown attitudes and behaviors illustrative of counter narratives. People are then asked what difference these unique outcomes have made or would make in their lives, thus strengthening the meaning of, and likelihood of, possible action. As in motivational interviewing, as the weight increases on the side of the counter story, the person becomes more determined to carry the new story forward and thus enters the action stage.

ACTION: The action phase in mediation is when parties develop mutual understandings and produce agreements about how to go forward. This is a vulnerable stage in mediation as making public commitment to the counter narrative of cooperation is still susceptible to being overwhelmed by the conflict narrative lurking in the shadows. Progress forward is made when commitments are followed through and faithfully adhered to. Each new lived experience strengthens the cooperative narrative and leads to what Prochaska and his colleagues call the maintenance or 'holding' phase where a new relational narrative becomes embedded.

MAINTENANCE: In narrative mediation emergent counter narratives take hold in the presence of an audience. People directly or indirectly affected by the new agreements can strengthen the resolve of the parties previously in conflict. If, however, this audience does not support the changes, they can become aligned in an effort to undermine the change and destabilize new understandings. Agreements can quickly unravel in the face of resurgent problem-saturated forces and the narrative of cooperation is not maintained.

RELAPSE: In motivational interviewing this is described as a *relapse*, because old habits and behaviors return. A relapse signals a return to an earlier phase in the cycle of change, usually the contemplation stage. Relapses can be normalized, however, as a predictable aspects of change and sometimes people go through the stages three or four times before the new changes are established. In narrative mediation, we make no such normative predictions that individuals will cycle through numerous rounds of agreement and disagreement, although we do recognize that problematic relationship stories do often reassert themselves and require repetition of the steps in the process.

An astute narrative practitioner is realistic about the vulnerability of a counter narrative of cooperation to the pull of problem-saturated narratives, and of the cultural discourses that drive them. Plans need, therefore, to be made around *predictions of relapse*. When understandings and agreements are reached, narrative mediators often shift their focus from supporting change to raising questions about its chances of survival. The questions asked now change and need to focus on helping protect the emergent narrative. Here are some examples:

- *What could go wrong and how would you deal with it?*
- *If the conflict should return, what strategies can you employ to ward off threats to the understandings you have just made?*
- *What experiences have you had in the past that are worth remembering when new challenges present themselves?*
- *How will you resist the temptation to be pulled back into the conflict when things get tough?*

This chapter has been arguing that the practices outlined in earlier chapters have to be used with good timing as well as skill. It matters where people are in the process of change. At some points in the process, asking lots of curious questions to explore a conflict are important. At other moments, double listening for openings to a counter story are helpful. After people have started to move into a counter story of greater understanding or cooperation, the focus changes, and it makes little sense to go back to previous exploration of the conflict story. Instead, the mediator needs to inquire into what might grow and sustain a counter narrative.

As we close this chapter and end the book, we hope you will take away specific understandings of how to practice narrative mediation. To this end, we have explained the intentions behind doing things, provided suggestions for fruitful lines of inquiry, and laid out numerous illustrations of narrative work in conflict coaching, conferencing and mediation. Our hope is that people who are invited into these conversations find them ethically respectful and helpful in opening up new dimensions of experience. Our hope too is that practitioners will be inspired to apply these ideas within multiple settings: including schools, organizations, communities, families, and in healthcare fields.

References

Beaudoin, M-N., & Taylor, M. (2009). *Responding to the culture of bullying and disrespect* (2nd Ed.). Thousand Oaks, CA: Corwin Press.

Berger, P. L., & Luckmann, T. (1966). *The social construction of reality: A treatise in the sociology of knowledge.* Garden City, NY: Anchor Books.

Bruner, J. (1986). *Actual minds, possible worlds.* Cambridge, MA: Harvard University Press.

Burr, V. (2003). *Social Constructionism* (2nd Ed.). London, UK: Routledge.

Cobb, S. (1993). Empowerment and mediation—A narrative perspective. *Negotiation Journal, 9,* 245-259.

Cobb, S. (2012). *Speaking of violence: The poetics and politics of narrative dynamics in conflict resolution.* New York, NY: Oxford University Press.

Davies, B., & Harré, R. (1990). Positioning: The discursive production of selves. *Journal for the Theory of Social Behavior, 20,* 43–63.

Deleuze, G. (1988). *Foucault* (S. Hand, Trans.). Minneapolis, MN: University of Minnesota Press.

Deleuze, G. (1995). *Negotiations* (M. Joughin, Trans.). New York, NY: Columbia University Press.

Deleuze, G., & Guattari, F. (1994). *What is philosophy?* (H. Tomlinson, & G. Burchell, Trans.). New York, NY: Columbia University Press.

Emery, R.E. (1995). Divorce mediation: Negotiating agreements and renegotiating relationships. *Family Relations, 44,* 377-383.

Fisher, R., Ury, W., & Patton, B. (2011). *Getting to yes: Negotiating agreement without giving in* (Revised Ed.). London, UK: Penguin.

Foucault, M. (1972). *The order of things: An archaeology of the human sciences.* New York, NY: Pantheon.

Foucault, M. (1978). *The history of sexuality: An introduction: Vol. 1* (R. Hurley, Trans.). New York, NY: Vintage Books.

Foucault, M. (1980). *Power/knowledge: Selected interviews and other writings.* New York, NY: Pantheon Books.

Foucault, M. (1982). Afterword: the subject and power. In H. Dreyfus, & P. Rabinow (Eds.), *Michel Foucault: Beyond Structuralism and Hermeneutics* (Pp. 199–226). Brighton, U.K.: Harvester Press.

Foucault, M. (1989). *Foucault live (Interviews 1966/84).* (S. Lotringer, Ed. J. Johnston, Trans.). New York, NY: Semiotext.

Foucault, M. (2000). *Power: Essential works of Foucault, 1954–1984* (Vol. 3). (J. Faubion, Ed. R. Hurley, Trans.). New York, NY: New Press.

Geertz, C. (1983). *Local knowledge: Further essays in interpretive anthropology.* New York, NY: Basic Books.

Gergen, K. (2009). *An Invitation to Social Construction* (2nd Ed.). Thousand Oaks, CA: Sage.

Gougaud, H. (2000). *Contes du Pacifique.* Paris, France: Seuil.

Hedtke, L., & Winslade, J. (2004). *Re-membering lives: Conversations with the dying and the bereaved.* Amityville, NY: Baywood Publishing.

Kohn, L.T., Corrigan, J. M., & Donaldson, M. S. (2000). *To err is human: Building a safer Health System Committee on quality of health care in America.*

Washington, DC: Institute of Medicine / National Academy Press.

Longfellow, H. W. (2000). Table-talk. In *Henry Wadsworth Longfellow: Poems and other writings* (J.D. McLatchy, Ed.) (pp. 796-799). New York, NY: Library of America.

Lyotard, J-F. (1984). *The postmodern condition: A report on knowledge* (G. Bennington, & B. Massumi, Trans.). Minneapolis, MN: University of Minnesota Press.

Miller, W. R., & Rollnick, S. (2002). *Motivational interviewing* (2nd Ed.). New York, NY: The Guilford Press.

Monk, G., Winslade, J., & Sinclair, S. (2008). *New horizons in multicultural counseling.* Thousand Oaks, CA: Sage.

Moore, C. (1996). *The mediation process: Practical strategies for resolving conflict.* San Francisco, CA: Jossey Bass.

Morgan, A. (2000). *What is narrative therapy? An easy-to-read introduction.* Adelaide, AU: Dulwich Centre Publications.

Nelson, H. L. (2001). *Damaged identities; Narrative repair.* London, U.K.: Cornell University Press.

Pearce, W. B. (2007). *Making social worlds: A communication perspective.* Malden, MA: Blackwell.

Prochaska, J.O., DiClemente, C.C., & Norcross, J.C. (1992). In search of how people change. Applications to addictive behaviors. *American Psychologist, 47,* 1102-1114.

Restorative Practices Development Team. (2004). *Restorative practices in schools: A resource.* Hamilton, New Zealand: School of Education, University of Waikato.

Westmark, T., Offenberg, L., & Nissen, D. (2011). *Explorations: An E-Journal of narrative practice, 2011,* 21-35.

White, M. (1989). The externalisation of the problem and the re-authoring of relationships. In M. White, *Selected papers* (pp. 3-21). Adelaide, South Australia: Dulwich Centre.

White, M. (2000). Re-engaging with history: The absent but implicit. In M. White, *Reflections on narrative practice: Essays & interviews.* Adelaide, Australia: Dulwich Centre Publications.

White, M. (2007). *Maps of narrative practice.* New York, NY: Norton.

White, M., & Epston, D. (1990). *Narrative means to therapeutic ends.* New York, NY: Norton.

Winslade, J., & Monk, G. (2000). *Narrative mediation: A new approach to conflict resolution.* San Francisco, CA: Jossey Bass.

Winslade, J., & Monk, G. (2008). *Practicing narrative mediation: Loosening the grip of conflict.* San Francisco, CA: Jossey Bass.

Winslade, J., & Williams, M. (2012). *Safe and peaceful schools: Addressing conflict and eliminating violence.* Thousand Oaks, CA: Corwin Press.

Wu, A. W. (2007). Medical error: the second victim. The doctor who makes the mistake needs help too. *British Medical Journal, 320,* 726-727.

ABOUT THE AUTHORS

GERALD MONK

Dr. Gerald Monk is a Professor in the Department of Counseling and School Psychology at San Diego State University, an Associate of the Taos Institute, and a licensed Marriage and Family Therapist in California. Gerald also works as a founding partner, trainer, and consultant for MGL Healthcare Communications and Conflict Transformation to address high stakes conflicts when medical error occurs. Gerald worked as a psychologist and mediator in New Zealand for fifteen years prior to moving to the United States. Gerald has a strong interest in promoting constructionist theories and expanding the applications of narrative mediation. Gerald has taught numerous workshops on mediation in North America, Europe, Southeast Asia and the Middle East. He was a recipient of the Fred J. Hansen Grant for Peace Studies to conduct mediation workshops in Cyprus.

He has co-authored numerous articles and books translated in nearly a half a dozen languages. Some of the books include *Narrative Therapy in Practice: The Archaeology of Hope (1997)*, *Narrative Mediation: A New Approach to Conflict Resolution (2000)*, *New Horizons in Multicultural Counseling (2008)* and *Practicing Narrative Mediation: Loosening the Grip of Conflict (2008)*.

JOHN WINSLADE

John Winslade (PhD) is an Associate of the Taos Institute and a Professor at California State University San Bernardino. He teaches school counseling and is the Associate Dean of the College of Education at CSUSB. He was previously for ten years at the University of Waikato in Hamilton, New Zealand, where he still teaches part-time.

He has also taught mediation at California State University Dominguez Hills in an adjunct capacity. He is a regular contributor to the teaching programs of the Dispuk Institute in Denmark and the Conrad Grebel College at the University of Waterloo in Canada.

John has been a co-author of nine books on narrative therapy, narrative mediation and multicultural counseling, as well as many articles and book chapters. His work has been translated into Japanese, Korean, Chinese, Russian, Spanish, German and Danish.

His background includes working as a school counselor, youth worker, family therapist and mediator.

He is an experienced presenter who has taught narrative therapy and mediation in North America, Europe, Asia and Australia.

John Winslade can be contacted at:

jwinslad@csusb.edu